THE ✦ TIMES

TOP 100
GRADUATE EMPLOYERS

The definitive guide to the leading employers
recruiting graduates during 2017-2018.

HIGH FLIERS

HIGH FLIERS PUBLICATIONS LTD
IN ASSOCIATION WITH THE TIMES

Published by High Fliers Publications Limited
King's Gate, 1 Bravingtons Walk, London N1 9AE
Telephone: 020 7428 9100   *Web:* www.Top100GraduateEmployers.com

Editor Martin Birchall
Publisher Gill Thomas
Production Director Robin Burrows
Production Manager Nathalie Abbott
Portrait Photography Phil Ripley

Printed and bound in Italy by L.E.G.O. S.p.A.

A CIP catalogue record for this book
is available from the British Library.
ISBN 978-0-9559257-8-8

Contents

Foreword

By **Martin Birchall**
Editor, *The Times Top 100 Graduate Employers*

Welcome to the nineteenth edition of *The Times Top 100 Graduate Employers*, your guide to the most prestigious and sought-after employers that are recruiting graduates in 2017-2018.

Last summer's historic Brexit vote has turned the past year into a period of almost unprecedented political upheaval and economic uncertainty. In the turbulent aftermath of the UK's decision to leave the European Union, the Bank of England reduced interest rates to their lowest level in its 300-year history, the pound dropped to a 31-year low on the world's currency markets, and newly appointed Prime Minister Theresa May called a snap election to reaffirm her Government's 'strong and stable' leadership for the Brexit negotiations, only for the Conservative Party to lose its overall majority in the House of Commons.

As politicians, business leaders and the rest of the country continues to debate what form Brexit should take, it's still too early to have any real idea of the impact it will have on the UK's future, and recent economic indicators certainly paint a mixed picture about its effects so far.

Over the last 12 months inflation rose to its highest level for four years, in part because of last autumn's fall in the value of the pound, and the

> **"** *Since the first edition was published in 1999, more than a million copies of the Top 100 have been produced.* **"**

Bank of England pumped an additional £60 billion of funds to support the banking system through its quantitative easing programme.

But the latest unemployment figures are the lowest since 1975, with just 4.5% of the population out of work, and the proportion of unemployed 16 or 24 year-olds has nearly halved compared to five years ago. The stock market has fared well too, with the FTSE index of 100 leading companies reaching record highs in June this year, up more than 20 per cent compared with its pre-referendum level.

On university campuses though, there is little doubt that Brexit has already had a profound effect. Research with final year students from the 'Class of 2017' – 92% of whom voted 'remain' in the referendum – showed that up to three-quarters believed there would be fewer graduate jobs this year, as a direct result of the 'leave' vote.

This new mood of pessimism and disappointment meant fewer finalists made job applications to employers and more opted to stay on for further study at university or go travelling, instead of entering the graduate employment market.

And for employers, the last year has been a time of change too. Nearly half the organisations featured in *The Times Top 100 Graduate Employers* reduced their recruitment in 2017, bringing to an end four years of growth in vacancies for university-leavers.

If you're one of the 400,000 finalists due to graduate in 2018, then the more encouraging news is that employers featured within this edition of *The Times Top 100 Graduate Employers* are planning to maintain recruitment at a similar level to 2017, albeit with fewer vacancies available in certain sectors.

Since the first edition was published in 1999, more than a million copies of *The Times Top 100 Graduate Employers* have been produced to help students and recent graduates from the UK's top universities research their career options and find their first job. Eighteen years on, the *Top 100* continues to provide an unrivalled, independent assessment of the graduate employers that university-leavers rate most highly.

This year's rankings have been compiled from the results of face-to-face interviews with more than 20,000 final year students who graduated from universities across the UK in the summer of 2017. Students were asked to name the employer that they thought offered the best opportunities for new graduates. Between them, the 'Class of 2017'

named organisations in every major employment sector, from the top consulting firms, investment banks and technology companies, to the country's leading charities, engineering companies, public sector employers, high street retailers, the Armed Forces, media groups, property companies, and accounting & professional services firms. The one hundred employers that were mentioned most often during the research form *The Times Top 100 Graduate Employers* for 2017-2018.

This book is therefore a celebration of the employers who are judged to offer the brightest prospects for new graduates. Whether through the perceived quality of their training programmes, the business success that they enjoy, the scale of their graduate recruitment, or by the impression that their on-campus promotions have made, these are the employers that were most attractive to graduate job hunters in 2017.

The Times Top 100 Graduate Employers won't necessarily identify which organisation you should join after graduation – only you can decide that. But it is an invaluable reference if you want to discover what the UK's leading employers are offering for new graduates in 2018.

THE TIMES TOP 100 GRADUATE EMPLOYERS — Finding Out about the Top 100 Graduate Employers

IN PRINT

Each employer featured in this edition of the *Top 100* has their own **Employer Entry**, providing details of graduate vacancies for 2018, minimum academic requirements, starting salaries, and the universities employers will be visiting in 2017-2018.

ONLINE

Register now with the official *Top 100* website for full access to the very latest information about the UK's most sought-after graduate employers.

This includes details of employers' internships & work experience programmes, local campus recruitment events and application deadlines.

And get ready for your applications, interviews and assessment centres with up-to-the-minute business news about each of the organisations featured in this year's *Top 100*.

www.Top100GraduateEmployers.com

BY EMAIL

Once you've registered with the *Top 100* website, you'll receive **weekly email bulletins** with news of the employers you're interested in, their careers events at your university, and their forthcoming application deadlines.

ALDI

It's tougher than you think. Turns out I'm tougher than I thought.

Graduate Area Manager Programme

- **£44,000 starting salary (rising to £73,450 after four years) • Pension • Healthcare • Audi A4**
- **All-year round recruitment but places fill quickly**

The Area Manager role gives graduates real responsibility and fast progression. From day one, I knew that my skills, determination and strength of character were contributing to the success of one of the UK's fastest-growing supermarkets. Amazing when you think about it.
aldirecruitment.co.uk/graduates

BECAUSE I'M ALDI. AND I'M LIKE NO OTHER.

theguardian 2017/18 UK 300

THE TIMES
GRADUATE RECRUITMENT
AWARDS 2017
'Graduate Employer of Choice'
GENERAL MANAGEMENT

Go places

Become an ICAEW Chartered Accountant

Take your career to more destinations than you'd imagine as an ICAEW Chartered Accountant. With a focus on innovative thinking, ethics and leadership, you'll become a strategic business leader. And because ICAEW Chartered Accountancy is recognised and respected in 154 countries worldwide, you really can go places.

Learn more at **icaew.com/careers**

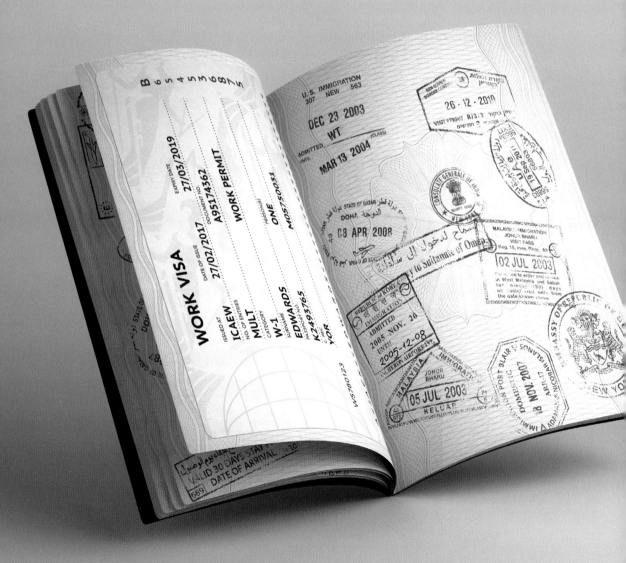

ICAEW

More rewarding

More global

AVERAGE GLOBAL SALARY
£49.9K
0–2 YEARS POST QUALIFICATION

ICAEW HAS 147,000 MEMBERS
الدوحة
48 147,000
WORKING IN 154 COUNTRIES

98%
OF THE WORLD'S 100 GLOBAL
LEADING BRANDS EMPLOY ICAEW
CHARTERED ACCOUNTANTS

EMPLOY ICAEW
91
OF THE TIMES
TOP 100
CHARTERED ACCOUNTANTS

ICAEW ACCOUNTANTS
ARE ON
78% OF THE BOARDS
OF FTSE
100 COMPANIES
AIJFPG

More respected

More sought after

More prestigious

ICAEW.
More than you'd imagine.

THE TIMES — TOP 100 GRADUATE EMPLOYERS — 2009-2010

THE TIMES — TOP 100 GRADUATE EMPLOYERS — 2010-2011

THE TIMES — TOP 100 GRADUATE EMPLOYERS — 2011-2012

THE TIMES — TOP 100 GRADUATE EMPLOYERS — 2012-2013

THE TIMES — TOP 100 GRADUATE EMPLOYERS — 2013-2014

THE TIMES — TOP 100 GRADUATE EMPLOYERS — 2014-2015

THE TIMES — TOP 100 GRADUATE EMPLOYERS — 2015-2016

THE TIMES — TOP 100 GRADUATE EMPLOYERS — 2016-2017

Researching The Times Top 100 Graduate Employers

By **Gill Thomas**
Publisher, High Fliers Publications

Despite all the uncertainty following last summer's Brexit vote, up to ten thousand employers – large and small – are set to recruit graduates from the UK's leading universities in the year ahead. Some offer formal development programmes for new graduates, whereas others are recruiting for entry-level vacancies which require a particular degree or qualification, but together they provide an estimated 200,000 jobs for university-leavers annually.

This impressive range of potential opportunities can make finding the organisation that is 'right' for you a daunting challenge. What basis can you use to evaluate so many employers and their graduate roles? How can you assess all the different options and decide which offer the best career paths?

There are few simple answers to these questions and no single employer can ever hope to be right for every graduate – everyone makes their own judgement about the organisations they want to work for and the type of job they find the most attractive.

So how then can anyone produce a meaningful league table of the UK's leading graduate employers? What criteria can define whether one individual organisation is 'better' than another? To compile the new edition of *The Times Top 100 Graduate Employers*, the independent market research company, High Fliers Research, interviewed 20,102 final year students who left the country's top universities in the summer of 2017.

Students from the 'Class of 2017' who took part in the study were selected at random to represent the full cross-section of finalists at their universities, not just those who had already secured graduate employment. The research examined students' experiences during their search for a graduate job and asked them about their attitudes to employers.

The key question used to produce the *Top 100* was "Which employer do you think offers the best opportunities for graduates?" The question was deliberately open-ended and students were not shown a list of employers to choose from or prompted in any way during the interview.

Across the full survey sample, final year students named more than 1,500 different organisations – from new start-up businesses and small local or regional employers, to some of the world's best-known companies. The responses were analysed and the one hundred organisations that were mentioned most often make up *The Times Top 100 Graduate Employers* for 2017.

It is clear from the wide variety of answers given by finalists from the 'Class of 2017' that students

> **THE TIMES**
> **TOP 100**
> GRADUATE EMPLOYERS

> *❝ In an outstanding achievement, PwC has been voted the country's leading graduate employer for the fourteenth year running. ❞*

TOP 100 GRADUATE EMPLOYERS
THE TIMES
The Times Top 100 Graduate Employers 2017

	2016			2016	
1.	1	PWC	51.	46	ASTRAZENECA
2.	4	CIVIL SERVICE	52.	NEW	DYSON
3.	2	ALDI	53.	91	CANCER RESEARCH UK
4.	3	TEACH FIRST	54.	68	AIRBUS
5.	5	GOOGLE	55.	63	SANTANDER
6.	7	DELOITTE	56.	83	SIEMENS
7.	8	NHS	57.	51	EXXONMOBIL
8.	6	KPMG	58.	57	BAKER MCKENZIE
9.	9	EY	59.	59	CITI
10.	13	GSK	60.	64	VIRGIN MEDIA
11.	10	BBC	61.	49	WPP
12.	11	UNILEVER	62.	NEW	THINK AHEAD
13.	14	LIDL	63.	67	ROYAL NAVY
14.	12	J.P. MORGAN	64.	74	DLA PIPER
15.	23	ROLLS-ROYCE	65.	62	POLICE
16.	17	ACCENTURE	66.	76	NETWORK RAIL
17.	16	HSBC	67.	47	BT
18.	15	GOLDMAN SACHS	68.	58	NESTLÉ
19.	20	BARCLAYS	69.	55	MI5 – THE SECURITY SERVICE
20.	19	JAGUAR LAND ROVER	70.	71	BOOTS
21.	21	MCKINSEY & COMPANY	71.	NEW	CHARITYWORKS
22.	18	JOHN LEWIS PARTNERSHIP	72.	88	LOCAL GOVERNMENT
23.	26	BP	73.	90	FACEBOOK
24.	22	L'ORÉAL	74.	50	BAIN & COMPANY
25.	24	IBM	75.	99	BMW GROUP
26.	27	SHELL	76.	96	BLOOMBERG
27.	33	ARUP	77.	61	PENGUIN RANDOM HOUSE
28.	42	FRONTLINE	78.	66	BANK OF ENGLAND
29.	25	LLOYDS BANKING GROUP	79.	80	DIAGEO
30.	36	ALLEN & OVERY	80.	70	AECOM
31.	43	BAE SYSTEMS	81.	72	WELLCOME
32.	29	MICROSOFT	82.	65	DEUTSCHE BANK
33.	34	P&G	83.	94	SAVILLS
34.	35	RBS	84.	NEW	CENTRICA
35.	28	BRITISH ARMY	85.	60	DANONE
36.	45	MARS	86.	81	GRANT THORNTON
37.	53	NEWTON EUROPE	87.	82	HOGAN LOVELLS
38.	52	AMAZON	88.	73	ROYAL AIR FORCE
39.	31	MORGAN STANLEY	89.	NEW	GE
40.	37	BOSTON CONSULTING GROUP	90.	75	MOTT MACDONALD
41.	40	ATKINS	91.	NEW	WHITE & CASE
42.	44	APPLE	92.	92	UBS
43.	30	CLIFFORD CHANCE	93.	NEW	GCHQ
44.	32	TESCO	94.	79	LLOYD'S
45.	38	FRESHFIELDS BRUCKHAUS DERINGER	95.	84	OXFAM
46.	39	LINKLATERS	96.	78	NORTON ROSE FULBRIGHT
47.	69	HERBERT SMITH FREEHILLS	97.	85	IRWIN MITCHELL
48.	41	SKY	98.	98	MCDONALD'S
49.	56	SLAUGHTER AND MAY	99.	NEW	CMS
50.	54	M&S	100.	NEW	E.ON

Source **High Fliers Research** 20,102 final year students leaving UK universities in the summer of 2017 were asked the open-ended question 'Which employer do you think offers the best opportunities for graduates?' during interviews for *The UK Graduate Careers Survey 2017* used several different criteria to determine which employer they consider offered the best opportunities for graduates.

Some evaluated employers based on the quality of their graduate recruitment promotions, the representatives they met at employers' campus recruitment events, or their application and selection process. Others focused on employers' general reputations – their public image, business profile or commercial success – or looked at the level of graduate vacancies available within individual organisations.

Many final year students, however, used the 'employment proposition' as their main guide – the quality of graduate training and development an employer offers, the starting salary and remuneration package available, and the practical aspects of a first graduate job, such as location or working hours.

Regardless of the criteria that students used to arrive at their answer, the hardest part for many was just selecting a single organisation. To some extent, choosing two or three, or even half a dozen employers would have been much easier. But the whole purpose of the exercise was to replicate the reality that everyone faces – you can only work for one organisation. And at each stage of the graduate job search there are choices to be made as to which direction to take and which employers to pursue.

The resulting *Top 100* is a dynamic league table of the UK's most exciting and well-respected graduate recruiters in 2017. In an outstanding achievement, the accounting and professional services firm PwC has been voted the country's leading graduate employer for the fourteenth year running, with a total of 8.2 per cent of finalists' votes.

The Civil Service, best-known for the prestigious Fast Stream programme, has moved up to second place, its highest ranking for twelve years, overtaking the popular trainee area manager scheme at retailer Aldi, which is ranked in third place this year. Although it has increased its share of students' votes year-on-year, the widely acclaimed Teach First scheme – now the UK's largest individual recruiter of graduates – has slipped back to fourth place. And despite reaching the top three in the *Top 100* in 2015, the internet giant Google remains in fifth place for the second year running.

Each of the Big Four accounting & professional services firms appear within this year's top ten. Deloitte has moved up to sixth place, following three years of dropping back in the rankings, and has overtaken rivals KPMG, who are now in eighth place in the new *Top 100*. EY is unchanged in ninth place. The NHS is ranked one place higher this year but the BBC has dropped out of the top ten for only the second time since 2002.

Pharmaceuticals and consumer goods company GSK has climbed three places to tenth place, its best-ever ranking. Lidl, the retailer that joined the *Top 100* as a new entry in 89th place in 2009 and has climbed the rankings in seven of the eight years since, is now in 13th place. And Rolls-Royce, the engineering and industrial company, has climbed an impressive eight places to reach the top twenty for only the second time in nineteen years – its ranking in 15th place is its best-ever position.

There have been very mixed fortunes though for the leading City banking and financial institutions in this year's *Top 100*. Just six of the top investment banks remain in the latest league table and none have improved their ranking year-on-year. Among the other eight banking or financial institutions listed in the top graduate employers, only Barclays, RBS and Santander have moved up the rankings this year.

The highest climbers in the new *Top 100* are led by Cancer Research UK, which has jumped back up thirty-eight places to 53rd place, following a large drop in 2016. Industrial conglomerate Siemens, the BMW Group and law firm Herbert Smith Freehills have each climbed more than twenty places. Newton, the Oxford-based consulting firm, and online retailer Amazon are both ranked in the top fifty for the first time, in 37th and 38th place respectively. And Frontline, the children's social work programme, has moved up an impressive fourteen places to reach 28th place, its highest ranking so far.

There are a total of nine new entries or re-entries in this year's *Top 100*, the highest being for engineering firm Dyson, which has had a convincing return to the rankings in 52nd place, ahead of Think Ahead, the mental health charity, making its *Top 100* debut in 62nd place. The Charityworks graduate programme is a new entry in 71st place, and international law firm White & Case is ranked in the *Top 100* for the first time, in 91st place. Energy companies Centrica and E.ON

TORI – PROBLEM-SOLVING PERFECTIONIST

"I LOVE IT WHEN A CREATIVE PLAN COMES TOGETHER – IN THE KITCHEN OR IN STORE!"

BRING YOUR BEST. WE'LL DO THE REST.

both return to the *Top 100* this year, along with engineering company GE, GCHQ and law firm CMS, which is a re-entry in 99th place, its first time back in the league table since 2008.

Organisations leaving the *Top 100* in 2017 include Transport for London – which was ranked in 48th place in 2016 – Bank of America Merrill Lynch, the European Commission, British Airways, BlackRock, Credit Suisse and consumer goods company Mondelēz International. And two employers that were new or re-entries in last year's rankings – investment company Standard Life and accountancy & professional services firm BDO – have also dropped out of this year's *Top 100*.

In the nineteen years since the original edition of *The Times Top 100 Graduate Employers* was published, just three organisations have made it to number one in the rankings. Andersen Consulting (now Accenture) held onto the top spot for the first four years and its success heralded a huge surge in popularity for careers in consulting – at its peak in 2001, almost one in six graduates applied for jobs in the sector.

In the year before the firm changed its name from Andersen Consulting to Accenture, it astutely introduced a new graduate package that included a £28,500 starting salary (a sky-high figure for graduates in 2000) and a much talked-about £10,000 bonus, helping to assure the firm's

popularity, irrespective of its corporate branding.

In 2003, after two dismal years in graduate recruitment when vacancies for university-leavers dropped by more than a fifth following the terrorist attacks of 11th September 2001, the Civil Service was named Britain's leading graduate employer. Just a year later it was displaced by PricewaterhouseCoopers, the accounting and professional services firm formed from the merger of Price Waterhouse and Coopers & Lybrand in 1998. At the time, the firm was the largest private-sector recruiter of graduates, with an intake in 2004 of more than a thousand trainees.

Now known simply as PwC, the firm has remained at number one ever since, increasing its share of the student vote from five per cent in 2004 to more than 10 per cent in 2007 and fighting off the stiffest of competition from rivals Deloitte in 2008 when just seven votes separated the two employers.

PwC's reign as the UK's leading graduate employer represents a real renaissance for the entire accounting & professional services sector. Whereas fifteen years ago, a career in accountancy was regarded as a safe, traditional employment choice, today's profession is viewed in a very different light. The training required to become a chartered accountant is now seen as a prized business qualification and the sector's leading

TOP 100 Number Ones, Movers & Shakers in the Top 100

NUMBER ONES		HIGHEST CLIMBING EMPLOYERS		HIGHEST NEW ENTRIES	
1999	ANDERSEN CONSULTING	1999	SCHLUMBERGER (UP 13 PLACES)	1999	PFIZER (31st)
2000	ANDERSEN CONSULTING	2000	CAPITAL ONE (UP 32 PLACES)	2000	MORGAN STANLEY (34th)
2001	ACCENTURE	2001	EUROPEAN COMMISSION (UP 36 PLACES)	2001	MARCONI (36th)
2002	ACCENTURE	2002	WPP (UP 36 PLACES)	2002	GUINNESS UDV (44th)
2003	CIVIL SERVICE	2003	ROLLS-ROYCE (UP 37 PLACES)	2003	ASDA (40th)
2004	PRICEWATERHOUSECOOPERS	2004	J.P. MORGAN (UP 29 PLACES)	2004	BAKER & MCKENZIE (61st)
2005	PRICEWATERHOUSECOOPERS	2005	TEACH FIRST (UP 22 PLACES)	2005	PENGUIN (70th)
2006	PRICEWATERHOUSECOOPERS	2006	GOOGLE (UP 32 PLACES)	2006	FUJITSU (81st)
2007	PRICEWATERHOUSECOOPERS	2007	PFIZER (UP 30 PLACES)	2007	BDO STOY HAYWARD (74th)
2008	PRICEWATERHOUSECOOPERS	2008	CO-OPERATIVE GROUP (UP 39 PLACES)	2008	SKY (76th)
2009	PRICEWATERHOUSECOOPERS	2009	CADBURY (UP 48 PLACES)	2009	BDO STOY HAYWARD (68th)
2010	PRICEWATERHOUSECOOPERS	2010	ASDA (UP 41 PLACES)	2010	SAATCHI & SAATCHI (49th)
2011	PWC	2011	CENTRICA (UP 41 PLACES)	2011	APPLE (53rd)
2012	PWC	2012	NESTLÉ (UP 44 PLACES)	2012	EUROPEAN COMMISSION (56th)
2013	PWC	2013	DFID (UP 40 PLACES)	2013	SIEMENS (70th)
2014	PWC	2014	TRANSPORT FOR LONDON (UP 36 PLACES)	2014	FRONTLINE (76th)
2015	PWC	2015	DIAGEO, NEWTON (UP 43 PLACES)	2015	DANONE (66th)
2016	PWC	2016	BANK OF ENGLAND (UP 34 PLACES)	2016	SANTANDER (63rd)
2017	PWC	2017	CANCER RESEARCH UK (UP 38 PLACES)	2017	DYSON (52nd)

Source High Fliers Research

TERRORISM DESTROYS OUR WAY OF LIFE.
Help us destroy terrorism.

As Britain's signals intelligence agency, we gather and analyse data to understand and tackle threats to our country.

It's varied and challenging work, as terrorists, hackers and cyber criminals increasingly target our infrastructure, businesses and our way of life.

To combat them takes a diverse range of people who work collaboratively by combining their abilities, knowledge and insights, to stay one step ahead of the adversaries.

Whatever your skills and background, you have the potential to help protect the country. Find out how at **www.gchq-careers.co.uk**

 Various Opportunites

GCHQ

Make a complex world yours

firms are regularly described as 'dynamic' and 'international' by undergraduates looking for their first job after university.

A total of 214 different organisations have now appeared within *The Times Top 100 Graduate Employers* since its inception and over forty of these have made it into the rankings every year since 1999. The most consistent performers have been PwC, KPMG and the Civil Service, each of which have never been lower than 9th place in the league table. The NHS has also had a formidable record, appearing in every top ten since 2003, and the BBC, Goldman Sachs and EY (formerly Ernst & Young) have all remained within the top twenty throughout the last decade.

Google is the highest-climbing employer within the *Top 100*, having risen over eighty places during the last decade, to reach the top three for the first

time in 2015. But car manufacturer Jaguar Land Rover holds the record for the fastest-moving employer, after jumping more than seventy places in just five years, between 2009 and 2014.

Other employers haven't been so successful though. British Airways, ranked in 6th place in 1999, dropped out of the *Top 100* altogether a decade later and Ford, which was once rated as high as 14th, disappeared out of the list in 2006 after cancelling its graduate recruitment programme two years previously. The latest high-ranking casualty is retailer Sainsbury's, which having reached 18th place in 2003, tumbled out of the *Top 100* in 2016.

Thirty four graduate employers – including Nokia, Maersk, the Home Office, Cable & Wireless, United Biscuits, Nationwide, Capgemini and the Met Office – have the dubious record of having

THE TIMES TOP 100 GRADUATE EMPLOYERS — Winners & Losers in the Top 100

MOST CONSISTENT EMPLOYERS	HIGHEST RANKING	LOWEST RANKING
ANDERSEN (FORMERLY ARTHUR ANDERSEN)	**2nd** (1999-2001)	**3rd** (2002)
PWC	**1st** (FROM 2004)	**3rd** (1999-2001, 2003)
KPMG	**3rd** (2006-2008, 2011-2012)	**9th** (2015)
CIVIL SERVICE	**1st** (2003)	**8th** (2011)
BBC	**5th** (2005-2007)	**14th** (1999)
GSK	**10th** (2017)	**22nd** (2002-2003)
IBM	**13th** (2000)	**25th** (2017)
EY (FORMERLY ERNST & YOUNG)	**7th** (2013)	**20th** (2001)
BP	**14th** (2013-2014)	**32nd** (2004)
ACCENTURE (FORMERLY ANDERSEN CONSULTING)	**1st** (1999-2002)	**20th** (2014)
EMPLOYERS CLIMBING HIGHEST	NEW ENTRY RANKING	HIGHEST RANKING
GOOGLE	**85th** (2005)	**3rd** (2015)
LIDL	**89th** (2009)	**13th** (2017)
JAGUAR LAND ROVER	**87th** (2009)	**16th** (2014)
ALDI	**65th** (2002)	**2nd** (2015-2016)
MI5 – THE SECURITY SERVICE	**96th** (2007)	**33rd** (2010)
TEACH FIRST	**63rd** (2004)	**2nd** (2014)
APPLE	**87th** (2009)	**27th** (2012)
ATKINS	**94th** (2004)	**37th** (2009)
NEWTON	**94th** (2013)	**37th** (2017)
BOSTON CONSULTING GROUP	**90th** (1999)	**37th** (2016)
EMPLOYERS FALLING FURTHEST	HIGHEST RANKING	LOWEST RANKING
BRITISH AIRWAYS	**6th** (1999)	**Not ranked** (2010, 2011, 2017)
FORD	**11th** (1999)	**Not ranked** (FROM 2006)
SAINSBURY'S	**18th** (2003)	**Not ranked** (FROM 2016)
THOMSON REUTERS	**22nd** (2001)	**Not ranked** (2009-2012, FROM 2014)
ASTRAZENECA	**24th** (2003)	**Not ranked** (2012-2014)
ASDA	**27th** (2004)	**Not ranked** (2016)
BANK OF AMERICA MERRILL LYNCH	**27th** (2000)	**Not ranked** (2017)
RAF	**32nd** (2005)	**Not ranked** (2015)
MINISTRY OF DEFENCE	**35th** (2003)	**Not ranked** (2007, FROM 2012)
MARCONI	**36th** (2001)	**Not ranked** (FROM 2002)

Source High Fliers Research

only been ranked in the *Top 100* once during the last fifteen years. And Marconi had the unusual distinction of being one of the highest-ever new entries in 36th place in 2001, only to vanish from the list entirely the following year.

One of the most spectacular ascendancies within the *Top 100* has been the rise of Aldi which joined the list in 65th place in 2002, rose to 3rd place in 2009, helped in part by its memorable remuneration package for new recruits (currently £42,000 plus an Audi A4 car), and was ranked in 2nd place in both 2015 and 2016. Teach First, which appeared as a new entry in 63rd place in 2003, climbed the rankings in each of the years following and reached 2nd place in the *Top 100* in 2014.

This year's edition of *The Times Top 100 Graduate Employers* has produced a number of significant changes within the rankings and the results provide a unique insight into how graduates from the 'Class of 2017' rated the UK's leading employers. Most of these organisations are featured in the 'Employer Entry' section of this book – from page 53 onwards, you can see a two-page profile for each graduate employer, listed alphabetically for easy reference.

The editorial part of the entry includes a short description of what the organisation does, its opportunities for graduates and its recruitment programme for 2017-2018. A fact file for each employer gives details of the business functions that graduates are recruited for, the number of graduate vacancies on offer, likely starting salaries for 2018, their minimum academic requirements, application deadlines, the universities that the employer is intending to visit during the year, plus details of their graduate recruitment website and how to follow the employer on social media.

If you would like to find out more about any of the employers featured in *The Times Top 100 Graduate Employers*, then simply register with **www.Top100GraduateEmployers.com** – the official website showcasing the latest news and information about *Top 100* organisations.

Registration is entirely free and as well as being able to access the website, you'll receive regular email updates about the employers you are most interested in – this includes details of the careers events they're holding at your university during the year, up-and-coming job application deadlines, and the very latest business news about the organisations.

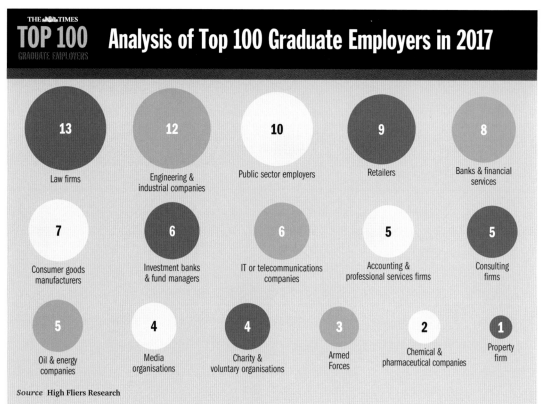

THE TIMES TOP 100 GRADUATE EMPLOYERS

Analysis of Top 100 Graduate Employers in 2017

13 Law firms	**12** Engineering & industrial companies	**10** Public sector employers	**9** Retailers	**8** Banks & financial services
7 Consumer goods manufacturers	**6** Investment banks & fund managers	**6** IT or telecommunications companies	**5** Accounting & professional services firms	**5** Consulting firms
5 Oil & energy companies	**4** Media organisations	**4** Charity & voluntary organisations	**3** Armed Forces	**2** Chemical & pharmaceutical companies / **1** Property firm

Source High Fliers Research

Sometimes it pays to get in early.

Early birds are often rewarded. And thanks to Launch Pad, you could be securing a future in Audit, Tax, Consultancy, Deal Advisory, Technology or Business Services sooner than you think.

Launch Pad is a new approach to graduate recruitment: a one-day event at the final stage of our process, it could see you being offered a role within as little as two working days. An interactive experience, it will give you the opportunity to demonstrate your talents through assessment activities and interviews with senior members of our team. Plus, you'll gain new skills, meet lots of people and find out more about the many opportunities at KPMG in the UK. Apply now.

kpmgcareers.co.uk/graduates

Anticipate tomorrow. Deliver today.

THE TIMES
TOP 100
GRADUATE EMPLOYERS

The Top 10 Graduate Employers 2002-2016

2002
1. ACCENTURE
2. PRICEWATERHOUSECOOPERS
3. ANDERSEN
4. CIVIL SERVICE
5. BRITISH ARMY
6. KPMG
7. UNILEVER
8. PROCTER & GAMBLE
9. GOLDMAN SACHS
10. MARS

2003
1. CIVIL SERVICE
2. ACCENTURE
3. PRICEWATERHOUSECOOPERS
4. BRITISH ARMY
5. KPMG
6. HSBC
7. BBC
8. PROCTER & GAMBLE
9. NHS
10. DELOITTE & TOUCHE

2004
1. PRICEWATERHOUSECOOPERS
2. CIVIL SERVICE
3. ACCENTURE
4. KPMG
5. NHS
6. BBC
7. BRITISH ARMY
8. PROCTER & GAMBLE
9. HSBC
10. DELOITTE (FORMERLY DELOITTE & TOUCHE)

2005
1. PRICEWATERHOUSECOOPERS
2. CIVIL SERVICE
3. ACCENTURE
4. KPMG
5. BBC
6. DELOITTE
7. NHS
8. HSBC
9. GOLDMAN SACHS
10. PROCTER & GAMBLE

2006
1. PRICEWATERHOUSECOOPERS
2. DELOITTE
3. KPMG
4. CIVIL SERVICE
5. BBC
6. NHS
7. HSBC
8. ACCENTURE
9. PROCTER & GAMBLE
10. GOLDMAN SACHS

2007
1. PRICEWATERHOUSECOOPERS
2. DELOITTE
3. KPMG
4. CIVIL SERVICE
5. BBC
6. NHS
7. ACCENTURE
8. HSBC
9. ALDI
10. GOLDMAN SACHS

2008
1. PRICEWATERHOUSECOOPERS
2. DELOITTE
3. KPMG
4. ACCENTURE
5. NHS
6. CIVIL SERVICE
7. BBC
8. ALDI
9. TEACH FIRST
10. GOLDMAN SACHS

2009
1. PRICEWATERHOUSECOOPERS
2. DELOITTE
3. ALDI
4. CIVIL SERVICE
5. KPMG
6. NHS
7. ACCENTURE
8. TEACH FIRST
9. BBC
10. ERNST & YOUNG

2010
1. PRICEWATERHOUSECOOPERS
2. DELOITTE
3. CIVIL SERVICE
4. KPMG
5. ALDI
6. NHS
7. TEACH FIRST
8. ACCENTURE
9. BBC
10. ERNST & YOUNG

2011
1. PWC (FORMERLY PRICEWATERHOUSECOOPERS)
2. DELOITTE
3. KPMG
4. ALDI
5. NHS
6. BBC
7. TEACH FIRST
8. CIVIL SERVICE
9. ACCENTURE
10. ERNST & YOUNG

2012
1. PWC
2. DELOITTE
3. KPMG
4. TEACH FIRST
5. ALDI
6. NHS
7. CIVIL SERVICE
8. ERNST & YOUNG
9. BBC
10. JOHN LEWIS PARTNERSHIP

2013
1. PWC
2. DELOITTE
3. TEACH FIRST
4. KPMG
5. CIVIL SERVICE
6. ALDI
7. EY (FORMERLY ERNST & YOUNG)
8. NHS
9. JOHN LEWIS PARTNERSHIP
10. GOOGLE

2014
1. PWC
2. TEACH FIRST
3. DELOITTE
4. ALDI
5. NHS
6. CIVIL SERVICE
7. KPMG
8. BBC
9. GOOGLE
10. JOHN LEWIS PARTNERSHIP

2015
1. PWC
2. ALDI
3. GOOGLE
4. TEACH FIRST
5. CIVIL SERVICE
6. DELOITTE
7. NHS
8. EY
9. KPMG
10. BBC

2016
1. PWC
2. ALDI
3. TEACH FIRST
4. CIVIL SERVICE
5. GOOGLE
6. KPMG
7. DELOITTE
8. NHS
9. EY
10. BBC

Source High Fliers Research

DRIVERS WANTED

To take us in new directions. To steer our future. To help drive new ideas forward.

At HSBC, we're looking for forward-thinking, perceptive and motivated people to join our Global Graduate Programmes, to help fulfil our customers' hopes, dreams and ambitions. Along the road, we'll help guide and encourage you to explore new paths and support you on your own journey.

Are you ready to take the wheel?

PROGRESSIVE MINDS APPLY

hsbc.com/careers

HSBC

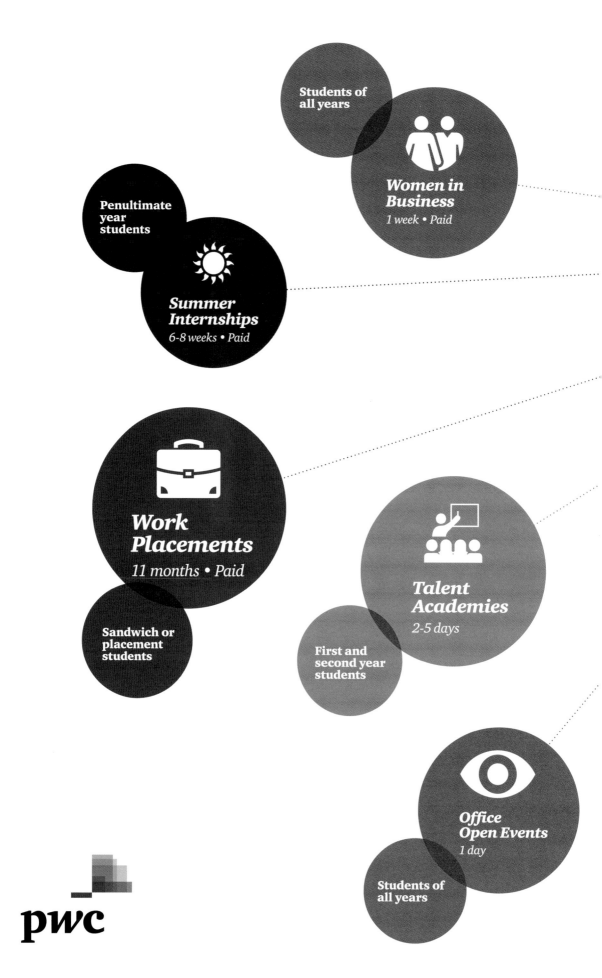

Boost your employability

The experience stays with you

We've got lots of different work experience programmes for every year of study, so you can learn more about our business and boost your employability. They'll help you make an informed decision about which of our career opportunities is best for you. Some could even lead to a job.

Join us. We're focused on helping you reach your full potential.

Take the opportunity of a lifetime
pwc.com/uk/work-experience

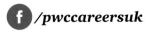 /pwccareersuk

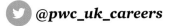 @pwc_uk_careers

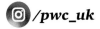 /pwc_uk

Valuing difference. Driving inclusion.

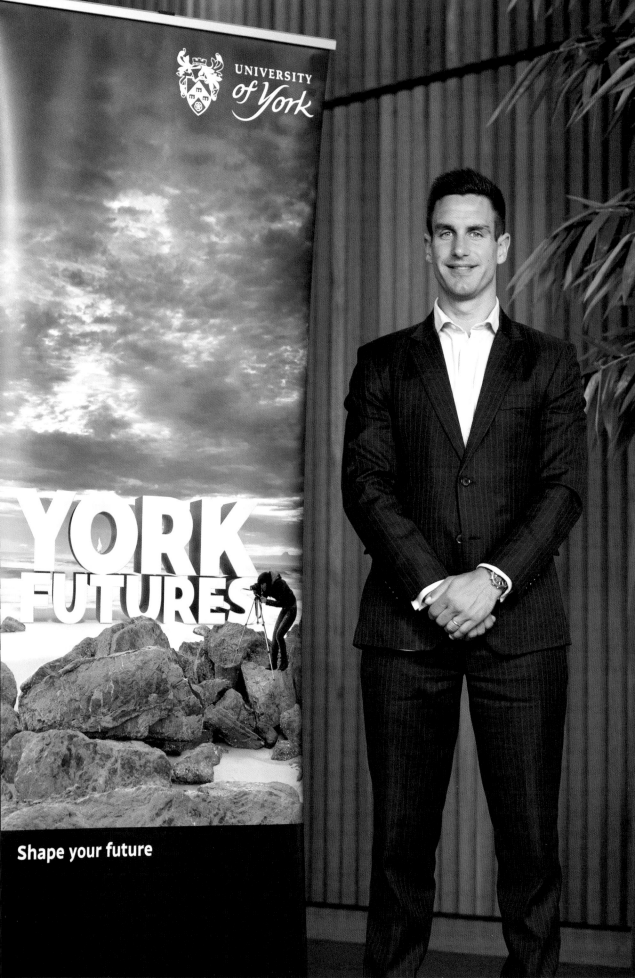

Successful Job Hunting

By **Tom Banham**
Director of Employability and Careers, University of York

Landing a place on one of the prestigious graduate programmes on offer from *The Times Top 100 Graduate Employers* has always been a highly competitive process. The sooner you can begin thinking about your options and researching different employment areas, job types and employers, the more likely you are to be successful.

When you first arrive at university, the autumn term is all about making the transition, meeting new friends and adjusting to a completely different way of working. But by the spring and summer in your first year, you'll be settled into university life and that's the time to begin exploring what it is you might want to do in the future.

Quite a number of employers run insight days, office visits or work shadowing specifically for first years around Easter time, so if you're not thinking about your options early, you'll miss those opportunities. To help you make the right career decisions, getting as many experiences as possible at university, as early on as possible, is key.

The first step is to try and work out what it is that really motivates you and where your passions lie. Do you enjoy problem-solving? Are you better at collaborating and working groups than on your own? And what are your main strengths

" Almost every organisation featured in the Top 100 will expect you to have had some form of work experience whilst at university. "

and values? Now would be a good time to speak to someone at your university careers service. Every university in the UK has its own local careers service, providing a wide range of resources and activities to support your job hunting and career decision-making, online and on their premises.

Don't be embarrassed if you're not sure what you want to do after university; your careers service will be very keen to point you in the right direction, and most offer pre-booked, bespoke guidance appointments with careers advisers, as well as shorter drop-in appointments for specific careers questions.

You could also talk to your academic tutor or lecturer to find out the types of careers that past students from your course have gone on to. Universities generally have very strong alumni relations departments who can put you in touch with recent graduates from your degree, to help inspire you with the career paths they've taken.

To discover more about specific industries, business sectors and job types, there's a wealth of information available online, through careers websites and jobs boards like *TARGETjobs*, *Prospects* and *Milkround*. And when you're ready to start discovering more about individual organisations, many of the best-known employers

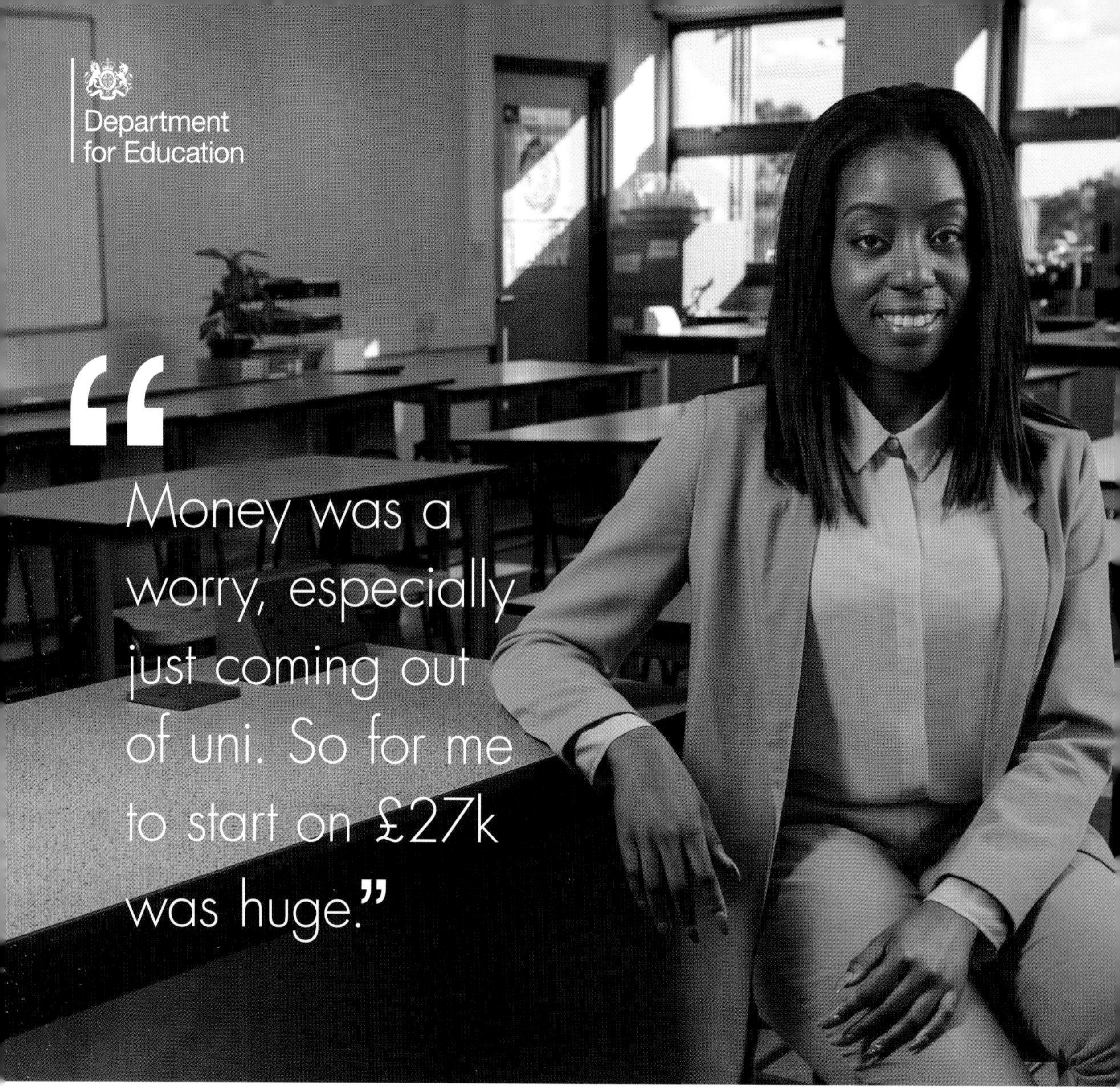

Department for Education
"Money was a worry, especially just coming out of uni. So for me to start on £27k was huge."

I'm Miss Bent. **I chose to teach.**

As a new teacher, you'll start on a minimum salary of £22k–£28k.*

Apply now to train in September.
Visit: education.gov.uk/graduates

TEACHING
YOUR FUTURE | THEIR FUTURE

*Subject to location. Figures are correct as of July 2017.

may well be visiting your university during the year to take part in local careers fairs or campus recruitment presentations.

To get the most out of these events, preparation is key because employers expect you to ask questions that are pertinent and relevant to their organisation. Don't ask about something which is already explained on their recruitment website and if you've not heard of a company, don't waste time by asking their head of graduate recruitment 'well, what do you do?' and 'why should I come and work for you?'. It will make an impression, but not the right one. There will be plenty of pre-event publicity for fairs and presentations, so you should have ample time to find out which employers will be on campus, research what they do, and then decide who you'd like to meet.

Many employer presentations are now held as skills training workshops, which means that you not only hear about their graduate programme but they'll also offer practical guidance about their application or selection process, or training on a particular business skill.

Almost every organisation featured in *The Times Top 100 Graduate Employers* will expect you to have had some form of work experience whilst at university. Many offer formal internships or a placement year and often use these experiences

as part of their graduate recruitment process, offering places on their graduate programme to students who perform really well during the work experience. It's a try-before-you-buy situation, both for you and the employer, and could mean that you get a definite job offer up to a year before you're due to finish your degree.

Internships usually take place in the summer between your penultimate and final year at university, so the time to be applying is in July or August after you've completed your first year. This might seem very early, but quite a few well-known employers hire at least 50% of their graduate intake via their internship programme. So if you miss out on the internships and end up applying to them in your final year, you've already halved your chances of being able to work for them.

But it's important to remember that even if you don't manage to get a place on a formal internship or placement scheme, there are plenty of other types of work experience that will be just as valuable when it comes to getting a graduate job.

Doing a part-time job during term-time or working during the university holidays – whether it's serving customers, being a team leader or doing a support role – can all help you demonstrate your resilience, the responsibilities you've had and how you've learnt from setbacks. Bear in mind, too,

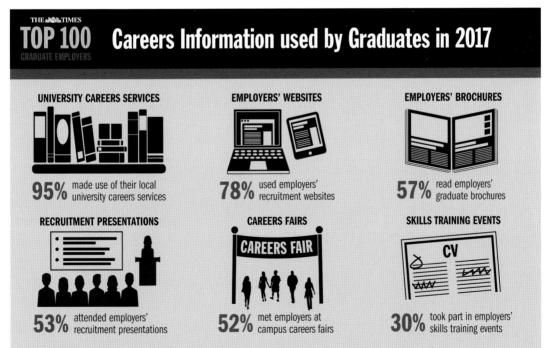

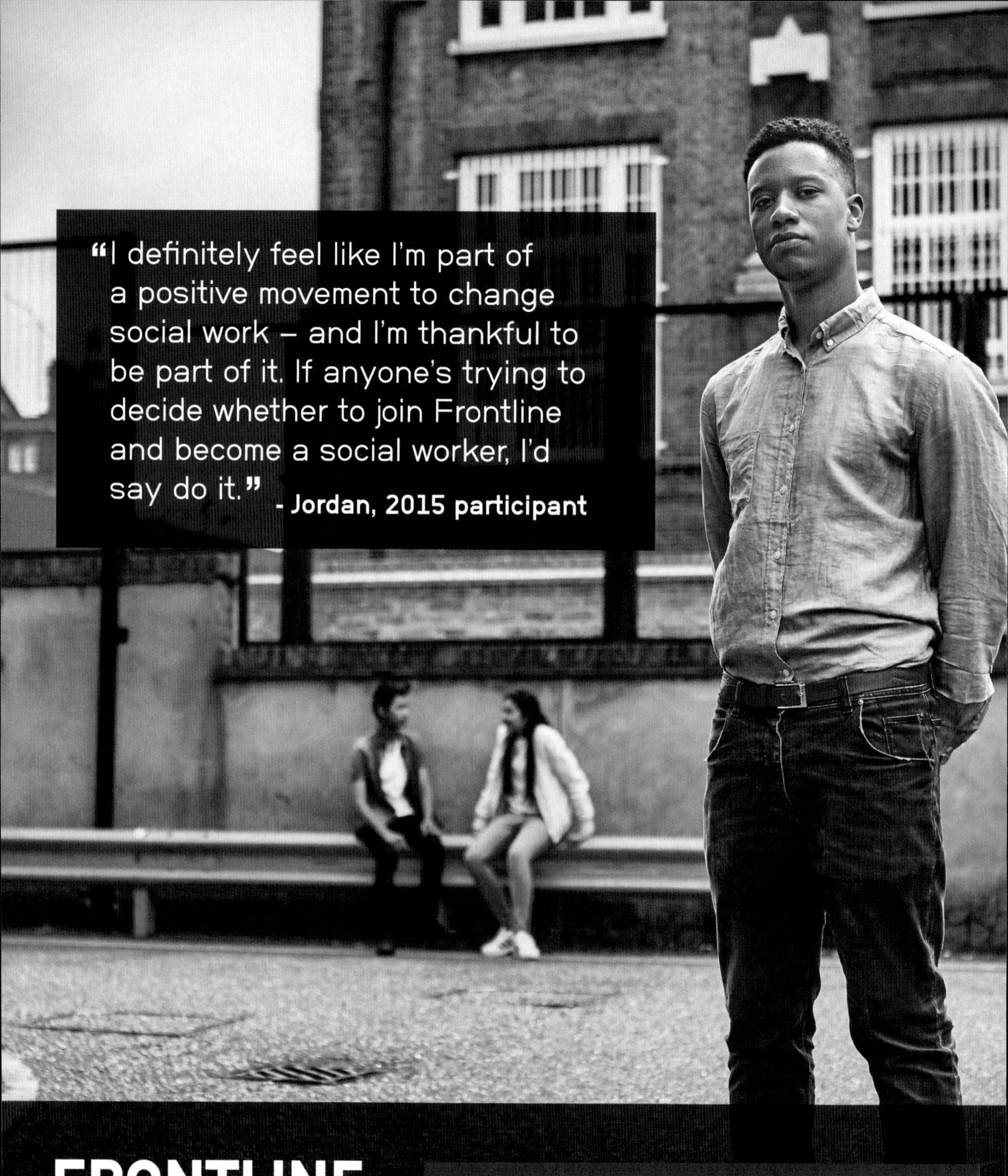

> "I definitely feel like I'm part of a positive movement to change social work – and I'm thankful to be part of it. If anyone's trying to decide whether to join Frontline and become a social worker, I'd say do it." **- Jordan, 2015 participant**

FRONTLINE

Frontline recruits outstanding individuals to be leaders in social work and broader society. On our intensive and innovative two year leadership development programme you will gain a master's degree and work to transform the lives of vulnerable children, young people and their families.

you can get similar benefit from the positions of responsibility you've had at university or through volunteering or doing charity work. Students who take the time to reflect on what they've done, understand those experiences and are able to articulate it, are the ones who really stand out to employers.

Whether you're making applications for summer internships, course placements or for a place on an employer's graduate scheme, the process is likely to be similar. The majority of online application forms will have three main parts, beginning with biographical data, which is where you list what you've achieved at university and also in your A-levels. Being honest about how you've performed in your first or second year is critically important. If you've not done as well as you'd anticipated, as long as you have valid reasons why then most graduate recruiters will be sympathetic, especially if it's because you've embraced other aspects of university life and had an array of other experiences.

The second part of the application form records your work experience. But this won't just be a list of what you've done and when you did it – it'll ask for the content, why you chose to do it, what've you've learnt from the experience, and how it's supported where you are today. That can take quite a bit of time to compile, especially to demonstrate the value of the experience, over and above 'I got paid'. Your university careers service can help you develop a narrative for this, so that it becomes a compelling reason why employers would want to invite you for interview.

The final aspect of the form will be competency or strengths-based questions. These can seem the most alien questions because they're focused predominantly on whether you have a certain skill or behaviour, such as leadership or effective team working. It's not just 'can you do it?' and 'have you experienced it?', it's your level of engagement and passion for something, which can be very hard to convey. Don't be tempted to bend the truth because it will quickly become apparent at interview stage if you don't possess those strengths. It's important that your application is authentic and really reflects who you are and what you're capable of.

If you're making a series of applications, be very wary about cutting and pasting between them. You may be able to transfer biographical details easily but the majority of the longer questions will have to be bespoke and specific to each employer in order to be successful. And remember, leaving

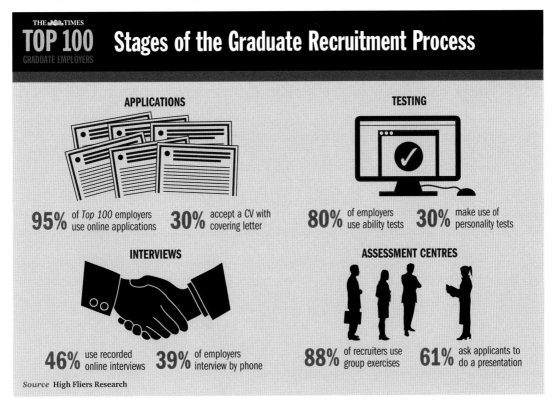

THE TIMES
TOP 100 Stages of the Graduate Recruitment Process
GRADUATE EMPLOYERS

APPLICATIONS

95% of Top 100 employers use online applications   **30%** accept a CV with covering letter

TESTING

80% of employers use ability tests   **30%** make use of personality tests

INTERVIEWS

46% use recorded online interviews   **39%** of employers interview by phone

ASSESSMENT CENTRES

88% of recruiters use group exercises   **61%** ask applicants to do a presentation

Source **High Fliers Research**

another employer's name in an application will almost certainly get you rejected, so make sure you check through your competed application for typos and errors before you submit it.

The next stage in the recruitment process is usually a set of online psychometric tests, taken either at the same time as the initial application or shortly afterwards. These could include personality tests, situational judgement tests or numerical or verbal reasoning ability tests. If you're applying for a technical role, there may be diagrammatic or inductive reasoning tests, too, that use a series of sequences and patterns to test your problem-solving capacity.

The number-one piece of advice is to do some practice tests beforehand. The majority of employers will have practice tests which you can try on their website and most careers services have a significant bank of psychometric tests that you can access and practice in your own time. Numerical tests are particularly common and are very similar to GCSE maths standard, so if you've not done any maths since then, they may seem quite tough.

If you do well in your tests, then you're likely to be invited for an initial interview. For some employers, this could be a traditional face-to-face meeting, but, for most, it will be a short telephone interview or, increasingly, an online recorded interview. These video interviews can seem very alien because it's a one-way, asynchronous and entirely impersonal experience. They're recorded through your laptop or PC and you'll have 20 or 30 seconds to prepare your answer for each question that appears on your screen.

It can seem very difficult and challenging because you don't know whether you're saying the right thing – there's no one on the other side to react to you and you can't gauge how well you're doing. Employers aren't looking for you to be a superstar news presenter but they will be assessing you for business credibility and whether you might be able to hold your own with their clients or customers. If you come across as pensive, nervous and you keep looking down at your notes, they may conclude you're not right for their organisation.

The final part of the recruitment process is usually an assessment centre or selection day. These are often held at employers' offices and include three or four different elements, such as a group exercise, a written exercise, a presentation

and personal interviews. Your careers service can help you prepare for each part of the day, through mock interviews and exercises, which will help you feel more confident about what to expect.

Be aware that you're probably being assessed from the moment you walk in the door and if you turn up late, that won't go down well. When you arrive, how polite you are to the receptionist can be fed back to the recruiters too. So as soon as you're in the building, you've got to take things seriously.

Your assessment centre interview could last up to an hour. To help prepare beforehand, make sure you have a copy of your original application so that you can refer back to it. It's likely to be either a competency or strengths-based interview and employers usually make it clear beforehand what form it will take.

At many assessment centres, the number-one deal breaker in terms of passing or failing the day will be how you problem-solve in a written exercise or presentation. You could have 30-45 minutes to work on a case study before making your recommendations in writing or in person. There isn't necessarily a right or wrong answer; recruiters are looking at how you take in information and apply that learning quickly to reach a conclusion.

Within the group exercise, a lot of people feel they have to be the leader and take on a role from *The Apprentice*. In reality, employers are looking for various leadership styles, so you don't need to be the dominant individual to be successful. But the key thing is that you do have to contribute something, because employers are assessing you based on the evidence you provide during the exercise. If you don't speak or participate in discussions, then you've pretty much failed.

Once you've completed the assessment centre, employers usually make a quick decision about whether to offer you the job. If you're in the fortunate position of being made offers by more than one organisation, think carefully about the experiences you've had with each employer and weigh up how closely their culture and approach matches your own values.

If you need more time to decide, most recruiters will be happy to give you this and will be keen for you to make the right decision. But don't be tempted to accept more than one offer at a time – you'll be taking up places that could have been offered to other graduates and may end up being left unfilled altogether.

Learn how to make a career plan that suits you and take action to make it happen.

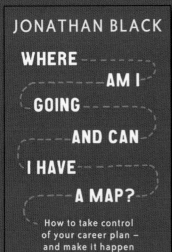

JONATHAN BLACK

WHERE
                 AM I
GOING
         AND CAN
I HAVE
         A MAP?

How to take control
of your career plan –
and make it happen

Where am I Going and Can I Have a Map? **is the positive and reassuring book by Jonathan Black, Director of the Careers Service at the University of Oxford, that will give you the confidence and skills to set about choosing your career.**

It distils the wisdom and experience of someone who advises and helps people work out their own career plan every week. It includes an extensive set of real life examples, and is grounded in statistics and sociological research where it is helpful.

To purchase the book, go to amazon

Deloitte.

Just BEAT it

Vincenzo Opeka from Risk Advisory at Deloitte is turning his idea into reality.

"It was a chance to shape a new product from its inception. I couldn't pass up the opportunity to take something new and exciting to our clients.

BEAT (Behaviour and Emotion Analytics Tool) is an outcomes based voice analytics application, which uses machine learning to analyse audio interactions.

Designed to help our Financial Services clients reduce the potential risk for mis-selling, the application 'listens' to different types of audio interactions and doesn't just analyse what a customer does or doesn't say, but also how they've said it and the emotions conveyed. For example, the application can identify potential vulnerability or confusion which allows organisations to intervene earlier and offer a different treatment for customers if necessary."

Discover more at deloitte.co.uk/imadeithappen

Nearly three quarters of student fear a lack of job opportunities

Students voice job market concerns

CONFIDENCE in th...

Top grads on £45k starter salary

Some of the count... leading employers for u... sity leavers are offering g...

Brex...'s ha... ill ... now ... worryi... ri...

Graduates 'offered £45k salaries

SOME of the country's leading employers for university... average salary closer to £30,000 during the next year. Britain's top employers expecting to expand t...

Top employers to take on more graduate

Greg Hurst Ed...

Britain's larg... plan to expar... university leav... sign of confid... The top 100... seeking to hire 2... ment program... more than last... It will be th... leading e... r graduate... for studer... ingly fo... pects since... ed to £9,00...

Brexit hits confidence in graduate prospects

t contract... l crisis in d dipped d steadily he larg... sts that not hit street ering ang... aduates sations ate pro... uits. rvey of

Top starting salaries

	Vacancies in 2017
Investment banking	
Law	789
Oil & energy	160
Banking & finance	
Consulting	691

Source: High Fliers Research

the 100 best-known graduate rec... by High Fliers Research, which ... employers t...

Confidenc in graduat job marke is dented, say expert

CONFIDENCE IN the grad... job market has worsened for... first time in five years, with... most three quarters of final-... students fearing fewer oppo... nities due to Brexit, a survey... found.

Brexit factor leaves students nervous over job prospects

When this summer's new graduates arrived at university three or four years ago, th... employers have decided to cut back. For final year students the impact of Brexit has been even more...

Students fear fewer jobs as a result of Brexi

CONFIDENCE in the graduate job market has worsened for the first time in five years, with almost three-q... ters of final-year students fearing fewer

and finance has dropped by up to a fifth in the past 12 months.

The survey, based on face-to-face in...

average student debt is now a record £37... Managing director of High Fliers Resea... ... all said: "Our latest survey shows j...

Graduates hit by jobs gloom

by **CATHERINE WYLIE**

Class of 2017 job nerves are calmed

The referendum result has not deterred graduate employers, reports Martin Birchall

Graduate confidence is hit by Brexit fears

FOR the first time in five years, graduate confidence in the job market has declined, with close to three quarters of final year students believing Brexit could affect their future

For the third year running, consulting is the top destination for new graduates, followed by entry level opportunities in marketing, the media and research and development. This contrasts with graduates

now quickly the impact of last year's Brexit vote has been felt by university students, 92 per cent of whom voted to remain in the EU. "Despite many of the country's best-known employers maintaining a business as usual

ver since last June's Brexit referendum, university

Understanding the Graduate Job Market

By **Martin Birchall**
Managing Director, High Fliers Research

When graduates from the 'Class of 2017' arrived at university three or four years ago, the big question for many was whether the new £9,000-a-year tuition fees – and the huge levels of student debt that they would bring – would be offset by better career prospects and a buoyant graduate job market.

Until 12 months ago, the answer would certainly have been 'yes'. Graduate vacancies at the UK's leading employers jumped by 16% between 2012 and 2016, starting salaries for university-leavers increased twice in three years, and the headlines about graduates' employment prospects were reassuringly upbeat.

But last year's Brexit vote brought this mood of optimism and growth to an abrupt halt. Although most of the country's biggest employers worked hard to maintain a 'business as usual' approach to their graduate recruitment, many final year students feared the economic uncertainty following the UK's decision to leave the EU would reduce the number of graduate jobs available in 2017.

Amidst the increasingly gloomy headlines, the reality is that the total number of graduate vacancies available at the country's top employers remained very similar to 2016 levels. But graduate recruitment at the leading investment banks, the

" The recruitment targets published by employers in this edition of the Top 100 suggest that graduate vacancies are set to dip a little in 2018. "

Big Four accountancy & professional services firms and other key employers in the financial sector was cut by up to ten per cent. And few organisations outside of the public sector stepped up their graduate intake this year.

In all, forty-six of the employers featured in *The Times Top 100 Graduate Employers* opted to reduce their graduate recruitment in 2017, making this only the second time in seven years that entry-level vacancies at the UK's best-known graduate employers haven't increased year-on-year.

The global financial crisis and the recession that followed in the UK in 2008 and 2009 had a profound effect on vacancies and graduate recruitment dropped by an unprecedented 23 per cent in less than eighteen months.

Although the graduate job market bounced back in 2010 with an annual increase in vacancies of more than 12 per cent, it took a further six years for graduate recruitment to overtake the pre-recession peak recorded in 2007. Graduate vacancies in 2016 were 32 per cent higher than in 2009, the low point in the graduate job market during the economic crisis, but just two per cent ahead of graduate recruitment a decade earlier.

For employers, this lengthy recovery has not been uniform or straightforward, and graduate

"There is a huge culture of investing in and developing young people in the company which I have benefited from first hand.

The amount of support I receive is immense and I am hugely grateful for it."

★ RATEMYPLACEMENT
2017 - 2018
**Top 100
Undergraduate
Employers**

**Social
Mobility
Champion**

INVESTORS IN YOUNG PEOPLE — GOOD PRACTICE AWARD GOLD

Standard Life   GRADUATE CAREERS

vacancies in seven key employment sectors – oil & energy, the City's investment banks, law firms, media organisations, financial services, and the Armed Forces – all remain lower than they were in 2007.

So what is the outlook for final year students due to graduate from university in 2018? The initial recruitment targets published by the employers featured in this edition of *The Times Top 100 Graduate Employers* suggest that graduate vacancies are set to dip a little in 2018.

Although nearly a third of *Top 100* employers are planning to take on a similar number of new recruits in the next 12 months, up to two-fifths expect to hire fewer graduates than they did in 2017, and just a quarter expect to expand their graduate intake in 2018. Together, the employers appearing in this year's *Top 100* are advertising 19,435 vacancies for 2018, compared to the 19,876 graduates hired in 2017, an annual decrease of 2.2 per cent.

The UK's leading accountancy and professional services firms are set recruit more graduates than any other sector, with vacancies for 4,200 new trainees in 2018. This is almost a quarter of the total number of graduate vacancies available at the *Top 100* employers.

The ten Government departments and other public sector employers that appear in the latest *Top 100* rankings are also planning to recruit more than 4,000 graduates in 2018, which is their biggest-ever graduate intake and the ninth time in ten years that recruitment of graduates has increased in the public sector.

By contrast, entry-level vacancies at the City's investment banks & fund managers have been cut by nearly a fifth and opportunities in financial services are down by 10 per cent. There are also almost a quarter fewer graduate jobs available in retailing, in part because of the cancellation of the graduate recruitment programme at one of the UK's best-known high street retailers.

Overall, employers in seven of the fifteen industries and business sectors represented within the *Top 100* expect to recruit fewer graduates in 2018, but several of the leading engineering & industrial companies and employers in the oil & energy sector are amongst those expecting to increase their graduate recruitment in the year ahead.

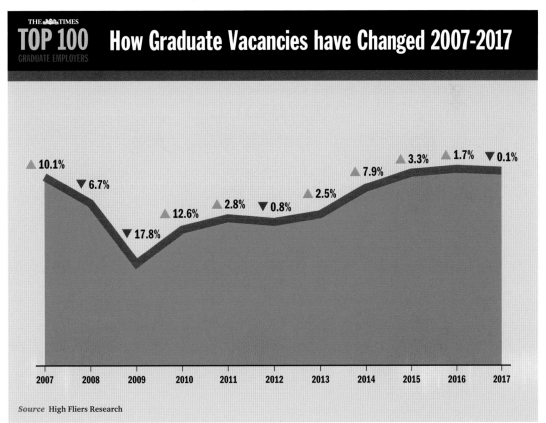

TOP 100 GRADUATE EMPLOYERS — **How Graduate Vacancies have Changed 2007-2017**

▲ 10.1% ▼ 6.7% ▼ 17.8% ▲ 12.6% ▲ 2.8% ▼ 0.8% ▲ 2.5% ▲ 7.9% ▲ 3.3% ▲ 1.7% ▼ 0.1%

2007 2008 2009 2010 2011 2012 2013 2014 2015 2016 2017

Source High Fliers Research

THE � TIMES
THE SUNDAY TIMES
Know your times

Subscribe and get 2-for-1 cinema tickets every weekend

Stay well informed with quality, balanced journalism every day on the subjects that matter.

Plus access to exciting offers and exclusive events.

For the latest student offers go to thetimes.co.uk/students

The rapid expansion of Teach First – the popular programme that recruits new graduates to work in some of the country's most challenging schools – means that for the sixth year running, its recruitment targets are the largest of any organisation in *The Times Top 100 Graduate Employers*, with 1,750 places available in 2018.

Other substantial individual recruiters include the 'Big Four' professional services firms – PwC (1,200 vacancies), KPMG (1,000 vacancies), EY (900 vacancies) and Deloitte (900 vacancies) – and the prestigious Civil Service Fast Stream (1,000 vacancies).

Half the employers featured in this year's *Top 100* have vacancies for graduates in IT, more than

two-fifths have opportunities in finance, and a third are recruiting for human resources positions or general management roles. At least a quarter of employers are looking for recruits to work in marketing, engineering, research & development or sales jobs, but there are fewer opportunities in retailing and more specialist areas such as transport or logistics, purchasing, property and the media.

More than eighty *Top 100* employers have graduate vacancies in London in 2018 and half have posts available elsewhere in the south east of England. Up to half also have graduate roles in the north west of England, the Midlands and the south west. Northern Ireland, Wales, East Anglia and the

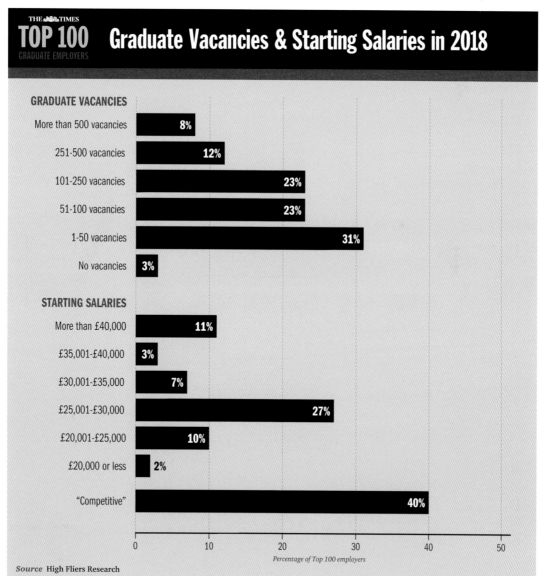

THE TIMES TOP 100 GRADUATE EMPLOYERS — Graduate Vacancies & Starting Salaries in 2018

GRADUATE VACANCIES

	Percentage
More than 500 vacancies	8%
251-500 vacancies	12%
101-250 vacancies	23%
51-100 vacancies	23%
1-50 vacancies	31%
No vacancies	3%

STARTING SALARIES

	Percentage
More than £40,000	11%
£35,001-£40,000	3%
£30,001-£35,000	7%
£25,001-£30,000	27%
£20,001-£25,000	10%
£20,000 or less	2%
"Competitive"	40%

Percentage of Top 100 employers

Source High Fliers Research

north east of England have the fewest employers with graduate vacancies.

Graduate starting salaries at the UK's leading employers have changed little over the last seven years. After annual increases every year until 2008, the average salary on offer from the country's top employers remained at £29,000 for four consecutive years, before increasing again in 2014 and 2015. The average starting salary in 2017 was £30,000 for the third year running.

More than half of the organisations featured in this year's edition of *The Times Top 100 Graduate Employers* have opted to leave their graduate starting salaries unchanged for 2018 but a limited number of employers have announced increases to their graduate pay packages – typically of between £500 and £2,000 each.

Two-fifths of the *Top 100* graduate employers simply describe their salary packages for next year as "competitive" but one in ten organisations – mainly investment banks, strategic consulting firms, City law firms, and one well-known retailer – are planning to pay starting salaries in excess of £40,000.

The most generous graduate package publicised within this edition of the *Top 100* is at Newton, the consulting firm, which is offering graduate salaries of between £45,000 and £50,000, with a starting-

work bonus of £3,000. Leading law firms White & Case and Baker McKenzie are offering new trainees salaries of £46,000 and £45,000 respectively. The retailer Aldi continues to pay its recruits a sector-leading graduate starting salary of £44,000 plus a fully-expensed Audi A4 company car, whilst close rivals Lidl now offers new graduates a salary of £40,000.

Up to half the UK's leading employers recruit graduates year-round, or in different phases during the year, and will accept applications throughout the 2017-2018 recruitment season until all their vacancies are filled. For employers with a single application deadline, most are in either November or December, although a limited number of organisations have October or post-Christmas deadlines for their graduate programmes.

Three-fifths of *Top 100* employers insist that applicants for their graduate schemes should have a 2.1 degree or better. A fifth specify a minimum UCAS tariff too, most in the range of 260 to 320 – the equivalent of 'BCC' to 'ABB' grades at A-level.

So, despite the continuing nervousness and concern about the impact of Brexit, for those who make the grade, there continues to be a wide range of career opportunities and some excellent starting salaries on offer from *The Times Top 100 Graduate Employers* in 2018.

THE TIMES TOP 100 GRADUATE EMPLOYERS
Graduate Vacancies at Top 100 Employers in 2018

	2017		NUMBER OF VACANCIES IN 2018	CHANGE SINCE 2017	MEDIAN STARTING SALARY IN 2017
1.	1	ACCOUNTANCY & PROFESSIONAL SERVICES FIRMS	4,200	▲ 1.8%	£30,000
2.	2	PUBLIC SECTOR EMPLOYERS	4,177	▲ 3.6%	£26,500
3.	3	ENGINEERING & INDUSTRIAL COMPANIES	2,275	▲ 5.5%	£27,500
4.	6	ARMED FORCES	1,600	▼ 8.4%	£26,000
5.	4	INVESTMENT BANKS & FUND MANAGERS	1,220	▼ 18.9%	£47,000
6.	5	BANKING & FINANCIAL SERVICES	1,140	▼ 10.2%	£30,000
7.	7	RETAILERS	985	▼ 23.8%	£30,000
8.	8	IT & TELECOMMUNICATIONS COMPANIES	905	▼ 7.5%	£30,000
9.	9	LAW FIRMS	870	▼ 2.1%	£43,000
10.	10	CONSULTING FIRMS	660	▲ 0.9%	£31,500
11.	11	MEDIA ORGANISATIONS	500	▲ 12.4%	£30,000
12.	13	OIL & ENERGY COMPANIES	285	▲ 7.5%	£38,000
13.	12	CONSUMER GOODS MANUFACTURERS	207	▼ 3.3%	£30,000
14.	-	CHARITY & VOLUNTARY SECTOR EMPLOYERS	171	NO CHANGE	£26,000
15.	15	CHEMICAL & PHARMACEUTICAL COMPANIES	150	-	£30,000

Source High Fliers Research

POVERTY.
AFFORDABLE HOUSING.
DOMESTIC VIOLENCE.
CLIMATE CHANGE.
SOCIAL CARE.

WHAT ROLE WILL YOU PLAY?

Charityworks.
Change the world
for a living.

Charityworks; Registered Charity No. 1136964, Company No. 7304744

Flt Lt Andrew Longbottom is an Aerosystems Engineering Officer in the Royal Air Force. His current role involves him being in charge of Typhoon aircraft. He joined after getting sponsorship from the RAF to complete his engineering degree and has been lucky enough to travel the world as part of his role.

"The Royal Air Force sponsored me through my undergraduate master's degree in Aerospace Engineering. Now I'm being sponsored through a master's degree, this time in Airworthiness."

"I have served on operational deployments in Afghanistan, Cyprus and the Falkland Islands, and have spent up to three months on exercises in Norway, California, Las Vegas – with 31 Sqn on Tornados and Oman with XI Sqn on Typhoon aircraft. I have also spent time in France, Denmark, Germany, Holland, Italy and Greece."

"I lead a three week, RAF sponsored, expedition to Chilean Patagonia. Leading a 6 man team, we completed the Torres del Paine National Park circuit, a 140km self-supported trek, in seven days before kayaking in the regions lakes and rivers wild camping as we went."

"The RAF has afforded me the opportunity to see and experience some amazing things, killer wales hunting and elephant seals birthing in the Falklands Islands, to kayaking amongst icebergs in Patagonia. But the best experiences have come from the sense of satisfaction and camaraderie when the team pulls together and completes a task which at first seemed almost impossible."

Flight Lieutenant Nosheen Chaudry is an Aerosystems Engineering Officer who has worked on several Squadrons including a GR4 Tornado Sqn at RAF Marham and on the Royal Air Force Aerobatic Team (RAFAT), The Red Arrows.

From early childhood Nosheen had a fascination with aircraft and the idea of flight. She was offered a RAF scholarship to be sponsored through Birmingham University to study engineering and now works around the cutting-edge aircraft used by the RAF.

"I fulfil a variety of roles, with responsibility for the teams maintaining aircraft within our fleet. It's challenging work but I like the fact I get posted from one station to another every two years to work on other related and sometimes different projects."

"One of the big attractions for me about the Royal Air Force is the sports and adventurous training on offer. I am really keen on athletics and have competed for the RAF Athletics Team for the last eight years." The RAF requires its personnel to keep physically fit and actively encourages adventurous training.

"I knew from an early age that this is the kind of thing I wanted to do and my family were very supportive in my career choice. In fact, they encouraged me to apply for the University Bursary which certainly helps with the cost of getting a degree."

For information about all of the roles available in the RAF, as well as sponsorship opportunities, visit the RAF Recruitment website. Search online for RAF Recruitment.

Graduate Careers in Law

By **Cathy Connolly**
Recruitment Partner, Slaughter and May

It's a real testament to the enduring appeal of careers in law that there are a record number of legal firms listed in the 2017 edition of *The Times Top 100 Graduate Employers* and more law firms than any other type of employer featured in this year's rankings.

Studying and training to become a professional solicitor is a lengthy and demanding process and there are two different routes available. For undergraduates who are studying a law degree at university, their next step is to complete the Legal Practice Course (LPC), before beginning a two-year training contract with a firm. For students who haven't studied law for their first degree, there is an additional year of study for the Graduate Diploma in Law (GDL), prior to starting the LPC.

Students often worry that if they haven't studied law, they'll be at a disadvantage to those that have, but that's not the case at all. Graduates who've studied other disciplines like engineering, classics, English and even medicine, help to bring greater diversity into the profession and a different way of thinking about things.

It's very positive for the firm and at Slaughter and May, we would typically recruit equal numbers of law and non-law trainees. And when new trainees

> **“During your two years as a trainee solicitor, you'll do a series of 'seats', spending time in different practice areas of the firm.”**

start, I really wouldn't know if they've done a law degree or not – everyone is on an even playing field.

To help students find out more about a potential career in law, we organise open days for first years but we don't expect anyone to make a decision about their future at that stage. We want people to come to university and enjoy university life for as long as they can without having to think about careers from day one. Formal work experience schemes are available during the second year, either at Easter or during the summer holidays, after which we accept applications for training contracts.

By the time you come to apply to any of the top law firms, either for a vacation placement or a training contract, it's essential to understand the differences between them. Each of the big corporate law firms is very different and you need to do your research carefully to make sure you understand the differences. Talking to your tutors and professors who may have experience of the firms may help, along with reading the firms' websites, brochures and entries in student guides.

If you spend time with a firm – through a university event, an open day or a vacation placement – the most important thing you should

ALLEN & OVERY

It's your heart going faster. Your knees going weaker. Taking that one big deep breath. IT'S TIME.

A career in Law

Our industry is changing faster than ever before. New ways of working create new opportunities, and we're looking for people who aren't afraid to challenge the status quo. If you want to realise your full potential, supported by a world-class development programme and mentored by some of the industries' leading experts, we want to hear from you. Search Allen & Overy Graduate to find out more.

A career in Law
Visit aograduates.com

🐦 @AllenOveryGrads   ⓕ /allenoverygrads   👻 AllenOveryGrads

be trying to get out of it is an understanding of the firm's culture. At Slaughter and May, we deliberately don't include formal assessments as part of the programme for the work experience scheme because we want everyone who comes to us to have the chance to work out whether it's the right firm for them or not.

I wouldn't advocate going from firm to firm to do multiple work experience schemes for your whole summer, but it may be useful to compare two different types of firms. Seeing how a larger law firm contrasts with a smaller firm, or perhaps a London firm versus a US firm, could be very helpful.

The selection process for a training contract at any of the top law firms is inevitably competitive. Our selection process includes a written exercise based around a business case study, and an interview with two partners that includes a conversation on a current affairs article. We're not looking for a particular type of person and we certainly don't want someone who just ticks a certain number of boxes – we recruit people who can think a bit differently and be innovative.

We are very open that we expect students to have a strong academic record and want those with a good 2.1 degree or above. But if someone has mitigating circumstances, then we would take that into account. We also understand that not everybody copes well in their first year at university, because it's quite a daunting experience and a complete change from school. That might mean your first year exam results aren't as good as they could be, so in that instance, we'd be looking for an upward trajectory through your time at university.

There's a myth that you have to have a First to be successful here but that's clearly not the case. You have to be bright because we work on the most challenging types of transactions and you need to have a certain level of intellect to be able to cope with that. But we're not just looking for 'brains on sticks', it takes a lot more than that to be a good lawyer. Being able to talk to people, explain concepts in a straightforward way, and using your common sense are just as important as the academic side of law.

Commercial awareness is another key aspect for prospective trainees. This doesn't necessarily mean reading the *Financial Times* from cover to cover while you're at university, but we do look out for students who are interested in what's going on in the commercial world and read the business pages of a reputable newspaper, listen to the news and listen to the radio. Knowing what's going on – not just in the world of current affairs but in the world of business too – and being able to discuss it is a big part of the selection process.

If you're successful and are offered a training contract, starting work as a new trainee can be something of a shock to the system. We expect trainees to be in the office by 9.30am and there may be conference calls and meetings earlier than that too. The most common questions are 'what are the hours like?' and 'will I be working until 2am every day?'. The answer is that it's completely variable – there will be times where you will be in the office late at night but that is balanced by down time when you won't be so busy.

Slaughter and May is unique among the 'Magic Circle' – London's elite group of pre-eminent law firms – in not having targets for the number of

THE TIMES TOP 100 GRADUATE EMPLOYERS

Training to become a Qualified Solicitor

LAW DEGREE
Usually 3 years

NON-LAW DEGREE
3 or 4 years

GRADUATE DIPLOMA IN LAW
1-year postgraduate conversion course

LEGAL PRACTICE COURSE
1-year vocational training, although can be done on a 'fast track' basis in 7½ months

TRAINEE AT LAW FIRM
2-year training contract, completing 'seats' in different areas of law

QUALIFIED SOLICITOR
Begin work as an 'associate' of a law firm

Source High Fliers Research

billable hours that our people do. Our lawyers only work late when necessary – there is no face-time culture at the firm.

You have to have a certain resilience to work in a big corporate law firm. If you're on a deal and it's running to a timetable, then you have to meet it and it can be tough. You can't come into a firm with rose-tinted spectacles and expect to be going home at 5pm each day. The best trainees are the ones that say at 3am, 'Right, there's four hours to go until we sign the deal, let's crack open the biscuits and Diet Coke and keep going'. There's a great sense of satisfaction when the deal has signed and you know that you will then have the opportunity to catch up on any missed sleep!

During the two years as a trainee solicitor, you'll do a series of 'seats', spending time in different practice areas of the firm, such as corporate & commercial, finance, tax, intellectual property or real estate. Your experience in these seats will help you decide which area of law you are most interested in and which area you will qualify into.

Once qualified you will become an associate of the firm and it's down to an individual really as to how long they take to find their feet – some associates may be doing more senior work within a year or two, whereas others might take longer to get to that point. At Slaughter and May, we don't have different levels of associate – so no junior associates or senior associates – and there is no set time as to when you can be considered for partnership.

Becoming a partner is a big step to take because, as a partner, you become an owner of a business and with that comes a certain amount of responsibility that you don't have as an associate. You take charge of client relationships, bring in new clients and drive the business forward. You're also responsible for managing the associates in your team, supervising them from a legal perspective as well as the pastoral side too.

Our people are our only asset – that's what a law firm is – so they are key to us and our future, which is why we work so hard to recruit, train and retain the very best talent we can. But not everyone who joins as a trainee will become a partner. Some will move to other firms or decide to become in-house lawyers – often for our clients – and others may move into other careers entirely.

For me, a career in law has always provided an exciting, rewarding job where no day is ever the same. When you come into the office, you won't know what's going to land on your desk. We do such a wide variety of work within each of our departments that 24 years after joining the firm, I'm still doing new things that I've never done before. I work with such bright people and being able to talk to them and discuss areas of law is just fascinating – it's stimulating and challenging and keeps you coming back for more.

THE TIMES TOP 100 GRADUATE EMPLOYERS — Law Firms featured in the Top 100 in 2017

	NUMBER OF GRADUATE VACANCIES	STARTING SALARY	TOP 100 RANKING 2017	NUMBER OF YEARS IN TOP 100
ALLEN & OVERY	No fixed quota	£44,000	30	19
BAKER MCKENZIE	33	£45,000	58	19
CLIFFORD CHANCE	80	£43,500	43	19
CMS	65	£26,000-£40,000	99	2
DLA PIPER	70	£27,000-£44,000	64	15
FRESHFIELDS BRUCKHAUS DERINGER	Up to 80	£43,000	45	18
HERBERT SMITH FREEHILLS	60	£44,000	47	16
HOGAN LOVELLS	60	£44,000	87	17
IRWIN MITCHELL	45	£25,000+	97	2
LINKLATERS	110	£43,000	46	19
NORTON ROSE FULBRIGHT	45	£44,000	96	12
SLAUGHTER AND MAY	80-85	£43,000	49	18
WHITE & CASE	50	£46,000	91	1

Source High Fliers Research

Law . Tax

CMS ACADEMY
THE NEXT GENERATION
VACATION SCHEME

DARING TO **DO THINGS DIFFERENTLY**

2017 saw the launch of the CMS Academy. It exposes you to clients, pro bono partners, industry thought leaders and the firm's global business. The CMS Academy challenges you more than any other vacation schemes in the legal sector.

This is what our 2017 CMS Academy participants had to say:

"It's a one off opportunity, there's nothing like this out there!"

"Truly exceptional experience!"

"Had the best three weeks!"

Excited? Find out more:

CMS UK Graduates #CMS Academy cmsgraduates **graduates.cms-cmck.com**

THE TIMES

TOP 100

GRADUATE EMPLOYERS

EMPLOYER	TOP 100 RANKING	Accountancy	Consulting	Engineering	Finance	General Management	Human Resources	Investment Banking	IT	Law	Logistics	Marketing	Media	Property	Purchasing	Research & Development	Retailing	Sales	Other	NUMBER OF VACANCIES	PAGE
IRWIN MITCHELL	97									●										45	140
JAGUAR LAND ROVER	20	●		●	●		●		●		●	●		●	●	●				250-300	142
J.P. MORGAN	14				●		●	●	●											400+	144
KPMG	8	●	●		●	●	●		●		●									Around 1,000	146
L'ORÉAL	24				●							●	●					●		28	148
LIDL	13				●						●	●		●			●	●		250+	150
LINKLATERS	46									●										110	152
LLOYD'S	94				●				●	●		●								10	154
LLOYDS BANKING GROUP	29	●	●		●	●	●	●	●	●								●		300+	156
M&S	50				●	●	●		●			●	●	●	●	●	●			200	158
MARS	36			●	●	●	●	●		●		●	●		●	●				35-40	160
MCDONALD'S	98					●														50	162
MCKINSEY & COMPANY	21		●																	No fixed quota	164
MI5 – THE SECURITY SERVICE	69				●				●											150	166
MORGAN STANLEY	39				●		●	●	●											200+	168
MOTT MACDONALD	90		●	●										●						250	170
NESTLÉ	68			●	●	●	●				●	●						●		25	172
NETWORK RAIL	66			●	●	●	●		●		●			●	●					Around 175	174
NEWTON EUROPE	37		●																	40	176
NGDP FOR LOCAL GOVERNMENT	72	●			●	●	●		●	●				●	●	●				Over 150	178
NHS	7	●			●	●	●		●						●					200	180
NORTON ROSE FULBRIGHT	96									●										45	182
OXFAM	95	●				●			●			●	●		●	●				50+ (voluntary)	184
PENGUIN RANDOM HOUSE	77											●	●					●		20+	186
POLICE NOW	65																		●	350	188
PWC	1	●	●		●				●	●										1,200	190
ROYAL AIR FORCE	88	●		●	●	●	●		●	●	●				●		●			500-600	192
ROYAL NAVY	63			●	●	●	●		●	●	●		●		●					No fixed quota	194
SANTANDER	55			●	●												●			Up to 50	196
SAVILLS	83													●						90	198
SHELL	26			●	●	●	●		●		●	●		●	●					60+	200
SIEMENS	56			●	●	●			●					●	●		●			70-80	202
SKY	48				●				●			●								90+	204
SLAUGHTER AND MAY	49									●										80-85	206
TEACH FIRST	4																		●	1,750	208
TESCO	44			●	●	●			●			●	●			●				100+	210
THINK AHEAD	62																		●	100	212
UNILEVER	12			●	●		●		●			●	●			●				45-50	214
VIRGIN MEDIA	60			●	●	●						●				●				40+	216
WELLCOME	81			●	●	●	●		●			●	●		●					10-12	218
WHITE & CASE	91									●										50	220
WPP	61											●	●							1-10	222

GRADUATE VACANCIES IN 2018

accenture

ACCENTURE.COM/ TIMESTOP100

As one of the world's leading consulting and technology organisations, Accenture achieves amazing things for its clients every day – whether that's increasing profits, gaining a greater market share, redefining strategies, innovating with leading-edge technologies or offering better customer experiences.

Accenture examines a client's organisation to solve their toughest challenges working out how best to improve it using the latest technology and digital solutions, and implements agreed actions to bring about positive, lasting and profitable change. For Accenture, it's not just about coming up with great ideas, it's also about successfully delivering transformational outcomes for a demanding new digital world.

To manage the broad spectrum of challenges Accenture's clients face, their business needs to be diverse, which is why they've set up their organisation across five key business areas. These are Accenture Strategy; Accenture Consulting; Accenture Digital; Accenture Technology, and Accenture Operations. Combining unmatched experience and specialised skills across more than 40 industries has enabled Accenture to deliver ground-breaking solutions and new innovative technology that impacts millions of lives every day.

There are a variety of ways that graduates can join Accenture. Whichever programme they join, graduates will enjoy the perfect mix of intensive training, expert support, live project experience and great benefits.

Accenture has a strong Diversity & Inclusion agenda, focussed on enabling their employees to be themselves and use their unique talents to make a difference in the world. Graduates are encouraged to explore their passions, both in and out of the workplace, and nurtured to develop their skills.

GRADUATE VACANCIES IN 2018
CONSULTING
IT

NUMBER OF VACANCIES
500+ graduate jobs

LOCATIONS OF VACANCIES

STARTING SALARY FOR 2018
£Competitive

UNIVERSITY VISITS IN 2017-18
ASTON, BATH, BIRMINGHAM, BRISTOL, BRUNEL, CAMBRIDGE, CITY, DURHAM, EDINBURGH, EXETER, LONDON IMPERIAL COLLEGE, KING'S COLLEGE LONDON, KENT, LEEDS, LEICESTER, LONDON SCHOOL OF ECONOMICS, LOUGHBOROUGH, MANCHESTER, NEWCASTLE, NORTHUMBRIA, NOTTINGHAM, NOTTINGHAM TRENT, OXFORD, ST ANDREWS, STRATHCLYDE, UNIVERSITY COLLEGE LONDON, WARWICK, YORK
Please check with your university careers service for full details of local events.

MINIMUM ENTRY REQUIREMENTS
Relevant degree required for some roles.

APPLICATION DEADLINE
Year-round recruitment
Early application advised.

FURTHER INFORMATION
www.Top100GraduateEmployers.com
Register now for the latest news, campus events, work experience and graduate vacancies at Accenture.

accenture
ELIZABETH IS
PASSIONATE
ABOUT
AI
ENTERPRISE
FOOD
Elizabeth works within our emerging technology practice as an AI and Robotic Process Automation practitioner. And Accenture's healthy work/life balance ethos means she can also enjoy hiking, time with her nephews and building her own catering company to support the homeless, so she can truly be herself and make a difference.
BE YOURSELF.
MAKE A DIFFERENCE
Apply now at accenture.com/gradfutures

AECOM

www.aecom.com/uk-ireland-graduate-careers

grad_recruit.europe@aecom.com

twitter.com/AECOM
facebook.com/AecomTechnologyCorporation

youtube.com/AECOMTechnologyCorp
linkedin.com/company/aecom--graduates

AECOM is ranked as the number one engineering design firm by revenue in Engineering News-Record magazine's annual industry rankings. The company is a leader in all of the key markets that it serves, including transportation, facilities, environmental, energy, oil and gas, water, high-rise buildings and government.

AECOM is a global network of experts working with clients, communities and colleagues to develop and implement innovative solutions to the world's most complex challenges.

Delivering clean water and energy. Building iconic skyscrapers. Planning new cities. Restoring damaged environments. Connecting people and economies with roads, bridges, tunnels and transit systems. Designing parks where children play. Helping governments maintain stability and security. AECOM connect expertise across services, markets, and geographies to deliver transformative outcomes. Worldwide, AECOM design, build, finance, operate and manage projects and programs that unlock opportunities, protect our environment and improve people's lives.

The AECOM Graduate Development Programme lasts for one and a half years, and will provide graduates with full financial and development support towards their relevant professional qualification, an assigned mentor, regular residential training modules, an opportunity to work on live client projects, external training courses where required, and multi-disciplinary exposure.

AECOM are seeking applicants from around 35 disciplines, including civil, structural, mechanical, electrical, building services, industrial and sustainable buildings engineering, as well as surveying, project management, planning, ecology, and environmental, water and energy related disciplines.

GRADUATE VACANCIES IN 2018

CONSULTING
ENGINEERING
FINANCE
PROPERTY

NUMBER OF VACANCIES
350 graduate jobs

LOCATIONS OF VACANCIES

STARTING SALARY FOR 2018
£24,000-27,000

UNIVERSITY VISITS IN 2017-18
BATH, BELFAST, BIRMINGHAM, BRISTOL, CAMBRIDGE, CARDIFF, CITY, DUNDEE, DURHAM, EDINBURGH, EXETER, GLASGOW, HERIOT-WATT, IMPERIAL COLLEGE LONDON, LANCASTER, LEEDS, LIVERPOOL, LONDON SCHOOL OF ECONOMICS, LOUGHBOROUGH, MANCHESTER, NEWCASTLE, NORTHUMBRIA, NOTTINGHAM, NOTTINGHAM TRENT, OXFORD, OXFORD BROOKES, PLYMOUTH, READING, SHEFFIELD, SOUTHAMPTON, STRATHCLYDE, SURREY, SWANSEA, TRINITY COLLEGE DUBLIN, ULSTER, UNIVERSITY COLLEGE DUBLIN, UNIVERSITY COLLEGE LONDON, WARWICK
Please check with your university careers service for full details of local events.

MINIMUM ENTRY REQUIREMENTS
2.2 Degree

APPLICATION DEADLINE
Year-round recruitment
Early application advised.

FURTHER INFORMATION
www.Top100GraduateEmployers.com
Register now for the latest news, campus events, work experience and graduate vacancies at AECOM.

Airbus is a global leader in aerospace, offering the most comprehensive range of passenger airliners and civil and military rotorcraft. As well as having strong capabilities in military aircraft and cybersecurity, Airbus is also Europe's number one space enterprise.

Graduates at Airbus can take their first steps towards building a big career. Over the course of their programme, they can explore the breadth of the business through a series of rotational placements – allowing them to build the knowledge, experience and understanding needed to progress within the organisation.

Airbus' UK graduate programme is both structured and flexible. Why? Because Airbus is a strong believer in career mobility, as it allows the organisation and its people to move forward. So placements are tailored to suit each graduate's needs, as well as those of the business, encouraging individuals to take control of their own career. Add to that outstanding training and development, a comprehensive induction, various technical and business modules, and graduates have everything they need to succeed in either commercial aircraft or defence and space. While the majority of roles are engineering-based, Airbus also recruits people with degrees in everything from Materials Sciences and IT to Business and Finance.

Airbus' placements last between two and three years and are designed to accelerate learning development – helping graduates to discover new career paths and open their mind to the company's possibilities.

What's more, working alongside passionate and determined people, graduates will help to accomplish the extraordinary – on the ground, in the sky and in space.

GRADUATE VACANCIES IN 2018

ENGINEERING

FINANCE

IT

LOGISTICS

PURCHASING

RESEARCH & DEVELOPMENT

NUMBER OF VACANCIES
100+ graduate jobs

LOCATIONS OF VACANCIES

STARTING SALARY FOR 2018
£27,000
Plus a £2,000 welcome bonus.

UNIVERSITY VISITS IN 2017-18
ASTON, BATH, BRISTOL, IMPERIAL COLLEGE LONDON, LIVERPOOL, LOUGHBOROUGH, MANCHESTER, SWANSEA
Please check with your university careers service for full details of local events.

MINIMUM ENTRY REQUIREMENTS
2.2 Degree

APPLICATION DEADLINE
17th November 2017

FURTHER INFORMATION
www.Top100GraduateEmployers.com
Register now for the latest news, campus events, work experience and graduate vacancies at Airbus.

GRADUATE VACANCIES IN 2018
GENERAL MANAGEMENT
RETAILING

NUMBER OF VACANCIES
100 graduate jobs

LOCATIONS OF VACANCIES

STARTING SALARY FOR 2018
£44,000

UNIVERSITY VISITS IN 2017-18
ABERDEEN, ASTON, BATH, BIRMINGHAM, BRISTOL, CARDIFF, DURHAM, EAST ANGLIA, EDINBURGH, EXETER, GLASGOW, LANCASTER, LEEDS, LEICESTER, LIVERPOOL, LOUGHBOROUGH, MANCHESTER, NEWCASTLE, NORTHUMBRIA, NOTTINGHAM, OXFORD, READING, SHEFFIELD, SOUTHAMPTON, ST ANDREWS, STRATHCLYDE, SWANSEA, WARWICK, YORK
Please check with your university careers service for full details of local events.

MINIMUM ENTRY REQUIREMENTS
2.1 Degree
240 UCAS points

APPLICATION DEADLINE
Year-round recruitment

FURTHER INFORMATION
www.Top100GraduateEmployers.com
Register now for the latest news, campus events, work experience and graduate vacancies at Aldi.

With roots dating back to 1913, Aldi (short for Albrecht Discount) came to the UK in 1990 and customers were amazed to see a fantastic example of 'no frills' shopping. Aldi are now one of the UK's fastest-growing supermarkets and one of the world's most successful retailers.

All graduates enter the business on their Area Manager Training Programme. It's gained a reputation for being tough, and rightly so. Graduates have an enormous amount of responsibility very early on and after 12 months, they'll take control of a multi-million pound area of three to four stores. Graduates receive incredible support throughout their training, with a dedicated mentor and regular one-to-one sessions with talented colleagues.

It's the perfect introduction to Aldi and a superb foundation for future success. It gives graduates a wider lens to make critical business decisions later on in their journey. Two to three years into the programme, secondments are available with many graduates having the chance to spend time in other parts of the UK, the US or even Australia. After five or so years as an Area Manager, high-performing graduates can then move into a Director role within (for example) Buying, Finance or Operations.

Aldi is built on an attitude. It's about never giving up; always striving for smarter, simpler ways of doing things. They're a business with integrity: they're fair to their partners and suppliers, and everything they do is for the benefit of their customers and their people. They look for graduates who are incredibly hardworking with a positive, 'roll their sleeves up' attitude. Those who join Aldi will blend intellect with a practical, business-focused mindset as they achieve impressive results with a world-class team.

ALDI

I joined for the challenge.
But I'll stay for my future.

Graduate Area Manager Programme

- **£44,000 starting salary (rising to £73,450 after four years) • Pension • Healthcare • Audi A4**
- **All-year round recruitment but places fill quickly**

The Area Manager role gives graduates real responsibility and fast progression from day one. I mean, not many employers would ask you to run a multi-million pound business after 14 weeks.
But that's the beauty of Aldi. You'll need to be driven, determined and ready to work outside your comfort zone. In return, you can expect world-class training and support from a global retailer.
It's why the Grocer named Aldi 'Employer of the Year 2017'.
And why I wouldn't want to be anywhere else right now.
aldirecruitment.co.uk/graduates

BECAUSE I'M ALDI. AND I'M LIKE NO OTHER.

theguardian 2017/18
UK 300

THE TIMES
GRADUATE RECRUITMENT
AWARDS 2017
'Graduate Employer of Choice'
GENERAL MANAGEMENT

ALLEN & OVERY

facebook.com/AllenOveryGrads **f**   graduate.recruitment@allenovery.com ✉

linkedin.com/company/allen-&-overy **in**   twitter.com/allenoverygrads **𝕏**

www.aograduate.com

Allen & Overy is a leading global law firm operating in over 30 countries. It covers 99 per cent of the world's economy, working with companies, organisations and governments on issues of incredible scope and complexity. It's a pioneering, forward-thinking business; the only one to have topped the Financial Times Innovative Law Firm ranking four times.

A&O has been voted the TARGETjobs most popular graduate recruiter in law for the last twelve years. Trainees can therefore expect a rewarding experience that will prepare them for a career at the very pinnacle of the profession. In each of their seats they'll support a senior associate or partner, with exposure to work that crosses departments and borders – in fact, 71% of the firm's work involves two or more jurisdictions. Around 80% of trainees have the chance to spend six months in one of the firm's 44 overseas offices, or on secondment to one of its corporate clients – who include 87% of Forbes' top 100 public companies.

The legal industry is changing fast, and A&O is working to equip its people with the skills and knowledge they will need to operate in the legal landscape of the future. For trainees, this means an in-house training programme characterised by flexibility and choice – like the chance to take a litigation course alongside their rotations.

Built on the work of talented and motivated people, in a supportive and collaborative environment, A&O is dedicated to challenging the status quo and leading the way in commercial law. So whatever they've studied – and around half have a degree in a subject other than law – A&O helps its trainees develop into exceptional lawyers and learn to do work of the highest possible standard.

GRADUATE VACANCIES IN 2018
LAW

NUMBER OF VACANCIES
No fixed quota
For training contracts starting in 2020.

LOCATIONS OF VACANCIES

STARTING SALARY FOR 2018
£44,000

UNIVERSITY VISITS IN 2017-18
BATH, BELFAST, BIRMINGHAM, BRISTOL, CAMBRIDGE, CARDIFF, DURHAM, EDINBURGH, EXETER, KING'S COLLEGE LONDON, LEEDS, LEICESTER, LONDON SCHOOL OF ECONOMICS, MANCHESTER, NOTTINGHAM, OXFORD, SCHOOL OF AFRICAN STUDIES, SHEFFIELD, SOUTHAMPTON, TRINITY COLLEGE DUBLIN, UNIVERSITY COLLEGE DUBLIN, UNIVERSITY COLLEGE LONDON, WARWICK, YORK
Please check with your university careers service for full details of local events.

MINIMUM ENTRY REQUIREMENTS
2.1 Degree
340 UCAS points

APPLICATION DEADLINE
31st December 2017

FURTHER INFORMATION
www.Top100GraduateEmployers.com
Register now for the latest news, campus events, work experience and graduate vacancies at Allen & Overy.

ALLEN & OVERY

It's your heart going faster.
Your knees going weaker.
Taking that one big deep breath.
IT'S TIME.

A career in Law

Our industry is changing faster than ever before. New ways of working create new opportunities, and we're looking for people who aren't afraid to challenge the status quo. If you want to realise your full potential, supported by a world-class development programme and mentored by some of the industries' leading experts, we want to hear from you. Search Allen & Overy Graduate to find out more.

A career in Law
Visit aograduates.com

 @AllenOveryGrads   /allenoverygrads   AllenOveryGrads

amazon
we pioneer

GRADUATE VACANCIES IN 2018

ENGINEERING

FINANCE

GENERAL MANAGEMENT

HUMAN RESOURCES

IT

LOGISTICS

MARKETING

PURCHASING

RESEARCH & DEVELOPMENT

RETAILING

SALES

NUMBER OF VACANCIES
250+ graduate jobs

LOCATIONS OF VACANCIES

*Vacancies also available in Europe
and elsewhere in the world.*

STARTING SALARY FOR 2018
£Competitive
Plus a sign-on bonus and RSUs.

UNIVERSITY VISITS IN 2017-18
BATH, BIRMINGHAM, BRISTOL, CAMBRIDGE,
DURHAM, EDINBURGH, EXETER, GLASGOW,
IMPERIAL COLLEGE LONDON, LONDON
SCHOOL OF ECONOMICS, LOUGHBOROUGH,
MANCHESTER, NEWCASTLE, OXFORD,
ST ANDREWS, STRATHCLYDE, UNIVERSITY
COLLEGE LONDON, WARWICK
*Please check with your university careers
service for full details of local events.*

MINIMUM ENTRY REQUIREMENTS
2.1 Degree

APPLICATION DEADLINE
Year-round recruitment
Early application advised.

FURTHER INFORMATION
www.Top100GraduateEmployers.com
*Register now for the latest news, campus
events, work experience and graduate
vacancies at Amazon.*

Amazon works today to design and build an enhanced customer experience for tomorrow, because innovation and creation is part of their DNA. They are not bound by conventional thinking, and believe that the best inventions are those that empower others to pursue their dreams.

To realise that, they create, they challenge, they fail and they push boundaries to invent on behalf of their customers. Earth's most customer-centric company is looking for the world's most talented individuals to be a part of new technologies that improve the lives of customers, shoppers, sellers, content creators, and developers around the world. Amazon believe it is still day 1 for the opportunities of internet and technology to improve the customer experience.

Amazon gives graduates responsibility and hands-on training to help them succeed. They have opportunities available in many different areas; for example, Area Managers are in charge of a department within warehouses, also known as Fulfillment Centers. They manage the day-to-day operations to deliver on the targeted key performance indicators. They are also responsible for leading a team whilst driving process improvement within their area. Through their work, they continuously improve the service level Amazon provides to customers.

The Area Manager role is one of many opportunities for graduates to develop their career at Amazon. The operations network offers roles within Engineering, Finance, HR, IT, and Logistics. Amazon also offers opportunities in Retail, Finance, Design, and Amazon Media Group. There are software development engineering roles at Amazon's Development Centres supporting businesses like Amazon Instant Video and Amazon Data Services. They strive to hire the brightest minds from universities around the globe, and have various opportunities for graduates who believe in their mission and want to be part of the team.

What's behind the smile?

Innovative Solutions
Customer Obsession
Exciting Challenges

We get our energy from inventing
on behalf of our customers.

Lead from the front, do something that really matters, and put other people first. A British Army Officer gets much more from life than they ever would with a civilian career – becoming part of a tradition of leadership and selfless service that stretches back hundreds of years.

The journey starts at the Royal Military Academy, Sandhurst. Here, the Army will teach new recruits everything from fundamental skills – like outdoor survival and weapon handling – to big-picture military strategy and the theoretical elements of leadership. Completing the course, Army Officers commission as 2nd Lieutenants and commence specialist training for their specific role in the Army. The Army needs all kinds of people to work effectively, so Officers could learn anything from engineering to high-tech telecommunications to intelligence gathering. After training, Army Officers take command of a platoon of up to 30 soldiers; they lead by example and put their soldiers' needs before their own.

Army Officers train alongside fellow recruits from all backgrounds, building a true sense of comradery and making friends for life; relying on each other for support and encouragement. They have the opportunity to travel the world, from skiing in Europe, white-water rafting in the USA to being on operations across the globe. With the aid of leading technology and state-of-the-art equipment, the Army make a real impact and difference in the world.

To be one of the world's best forces, the Army needs to operate seamlessly as a team. And, to operate seamlessly as a team, they need top-class officers leading the way. That's why Army Officers receive world-class leadership training; it offers people with potential a focus for their ambition, a clear path for promotion and a place where they can truly belong.

GRADUATE VACANCIES IN 2018
ENGINEERING
GENERAL MANAGEMENT
HUMAN RESOURCES
IT
LAW
LOGISTICS

NUMBER OF VACANCIES
650 graduate jobs

LOCATIONS OF VACANCIES

STARTING SALARY FOR 2018
£31,232
After training.

UNIVERSITY VISITS IN 2017-18
ASTON, BATH, BIRMINGHAM, BRADFORD, BRISTOL, CARDIFF, DUNDEE, DURHAM, EDINBURGH, EXETER, HERIOT-WATT, HULL, IMPERIAL COLLEGE LONDON, LANCASTER, LEEDS, LEICESTER, LIVERPOOL, LOUGHBOROUGH, NEWCASTLE, NOTTINGHAM, READING, SHEFFIELD, ST ANDREWS, SURREY, YORK
Please check with your university careers service for full details of local events.

MINIMUM ENTRY REQUIREMENTS
180 UCAS points

APPLICATION DEADLINE
Year-round recruitment

FURTHER INFORMATION
www.Top100GraduateEmployers.com
Register now for the latest news, campus events, work experience and graduate vacancies at the British Army.

THIS IS BELONGING

WHERE REAL LEADERS BELONG

The opportunity to do something that matters. Building bonds that never break. A career full of adventure and accomplishment. You'll find all of this as a British Army Officer. We'll give you world-class training and state-of-the-art technology to use, so you'll achieve great things. You'll have a career steeped in tradition, filled with responsibility and rich with opportunity. You'll find a clear career path for progressing through our ranks and be awarded a starting salary of £31,232 (upon completion of training). And you'll develop into an exceptional leader, playing a key part in building the sense of belonging that empowers you and your team to accomplish anything.

Find where you belong. Become an Army Officer.

FIND WHERE YOU BELONG
SEARCH ARMY OFFICER

ARMY
BE THE BEST

careers.astrazeneca.com/students

facebook.com/astrazenecacareers **f**

linkedin.com/company/astrazeneca/careers **in**   twitter.com/AstraZenecaJobs **y**

instagram.com/astrazeneca_careers **O**   youtube.com/astrazeneca **YouTube**

AstraZeneca is a global biopharmaceutical business that pushes the boundaries of science to deliver life-changing medicines. Agile and purposeful, it annually invests over $5bn in R&D to pursue discoveries beyond imagination, and brings together 60,000 people in 100+ countries in a unique spirit of innovation.

Graduates from any discipline who are inspired by what science can do thrive in AstraZeneca's diverse and international culture. They take real responsibility from day one, and throughout their programme, they have the opportunity to contribute to ground-breaking projects and gain an extensive understanding of the global pharmaceutical industry.

There are many paths graduates at AstraZeneca can follow to achieve their career objectives. Outstanding personal development plans are devised with managers. Passionate leaders can be found at all levels. And there is a strong support network within a performance management framework which helps set graduates up for success. All within an energising and entrepreneurial environment.

Some programmes provide graduates with opportunities to work abroad. And as they explore their potential in a new location, they'll find that AstraZeneca is a company that offers a rich array of different experiences, perspectives and challenges.

Graduates at AstraZeneca work with bold thinkers whose ideas are as diverse as the cultures that have helped shape them. The company is proud to have gained a host of awards for its progressive working practices. It also recognises that diverse teams are innovative teams which strengthen the connections between employees, patients, stakeholders and the communities in which they work – all in a culture of collaboration.

GRADUATE VACANCIES IN 2018

GENERAL MANAGEMENT

IT

LOGISTICS

PURCHASING

RESEARCH & DEVELOPMENT

NUMBER OF VACANCIES
80+ graduate jobs

LOCATIONS OF VACANCIES

Vacancies also available in Europe, the USA, Asia and elsewhere in the world.

STARTING SALARY FOR 2018
£28,000+
Plus bonus, benefits and relocation (if applicable).

UNIVERSITY VISITS IN 2017-18
CAMBRIDGE, IMPERIAL COLLEGE LONDON, KING'S COLLEGE LONDON, LIVERPOOL, LONDON SCHOOL OF ECONOMICS, MANCHESTER, OXFORD, UNIVERSITY COLLEGE LONDON, WARWICK, YORK
Please check with your university careers service for full details of local events.

MINIMUM ENTRY REQUIREMENTS
2.1 Degree

APPLICATION DEADLINE
Varies by function

FURTHER INFORMATION
www.Top100GraduateEmployers.com
Register now for the latest news, campus events, work experience and graduate vacancies at AstraZeneca.

Exciting challenges on a global scale. How will you make a difference?

Start a career that will make a difference to people the world over. Take on real responsibility in a supportive, dynamic environment that's fuelled by innovation. Work with brilliant minds to solve important problems in areas of unmet patient need.

Our ambition is to deliver life-changing medicines to 200 million people – and in doing so, become a $50 billion company by 2025. We have opportunities for curious and creative, driven and determined graduates who share our passion for science on these Graduate Programmes in 2018:

- **Global Operations**
- **Information Technology**
- **Innovative Medicines & Early Development**
- **Pharmaceutical Technology & Development**

Whichever programme you follow, you'll have the opportunity to develop and excel in your chosen field. You'll find AstraZeneca is ideally placed to help you build a satisfying career, where learning, growing and meeting exciting challenges are all in a day's work.

As we build on our strengths to continue to meet the needs of a changing world, you'll be collaborating with people drawn from all backgrounds and cultures. This helps us to better reflect and understand our patients and the healthcare professionals we serve, in increasingly global markets – and ultimately, develop the medicines the world needs.

AstraZeneca welcomes applications from all sections of the community.

AstraZeneca is an equal opportunity employer. AstraZeneca will consider all qualified applicants for employment without discrimination on grounds of disability, sex or sexual orientation, pregnancy or maternity leave status, race or national or ethnic origin, age, religion or belief, gender identity or re-assignment, marital or civil partnership status, protected veteran status (if applicable) or any other characteristic protected by law.

To find out more, please visit:
https://careers.astrazeneca.com/students

MedImmune   AstraZeneca

As one of the world's most respected design, engineering and project management consultancies, Atkins is well placed to invest in the development of their graduates and they'll fully support them in becoming an expert in whatever inspires them most.

With Atkins, graduates will be joining a company that builds long-term trusted partnerships to create a world where lives are enriched through the implementation of their ideas. From moving people across London faster on Crossrail through to solving the energy challenges of the future, Atkins is the team creating a better future for us all. Their design, project management and engineering specialists are involved in some of the UK's most transformational projects.

Their people are experts in a wide range of sectors including aerospace, defence, education, energy, environment, information communications, transportation and water. They have a proud history in these sectors and an outstanding track record of success. But it's the future they're really excited about.

The world is facing some unprecedented challenges, and they're looking to draw on the talents of graduates to provide innovative solutions for clients in the public, private and regulated sectors. Atkins is always on the lookout for people who share their passion for problem solving; engineering graduates from civil, structural, mechanical, electrical, chemical, aerospace, systems and communications as well as IT, physics, geography and maths.

Atkins have designed a flexible framework that puts graduates in control of achieving their goals – whether that's gaining professional accreditation or simply building the skills needed for a successful long-term career.

GRADUATE VACANCIES IN 2018

CONSULTING
ENGINEERING

NUMBER OF VACANCIES
250+ graduate jobs

LOCATIONS OF VACANCIES

STARTING SALARY FOR 2018
£22,000-£26,500
Plus a £2,000 settling-in bonus.

UNIVERSITY VISITS IN 2017-18
BATH, BIRMINGHAM, BRISTOL, IMPERIAL COLLEGE LONDON, LEEDS, LOUGHBOROUGH, MANCHESTER, NOTTINGHAM TRENT, OXFORD BROOKES, SHEFFIELD, STRATHCLYDE, SURREY
Please check with your university careers service for full details of local events.

MINIMUM ENTRY REQUIREMENTS
2.2 Degree

APPLICATION DEADLINE
March 2018

FURTHER INFORMATION
www.Top100GraduateEmployers.com
Register now for the latest news, campus events, work experience and graduate vacancies at Atkins.

twitter.com/BAESGraduates

facebook.com/BAESGraduates

instagram.com/baesystems

linkedin.com/company/bae-systems

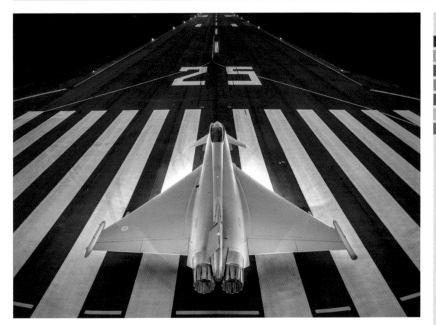

BAE Systems provides some of the world's most advanced, technology-led defence, aerospace and security solutions, employing a skilled workforce of some 83,100 people in over 40 countries. As one of the world's most innovative companies, they can offer an exciting and fulfilling career.

By demonstrating passion and enthusiasm to improve, graduates and undergraduates will receive the support needed to be creative and pioneering throughout their development to set the stage for an amazing future with BAE Systems.

The Graduate Development Framework (GDF) is a two-year scheme which develops people who are passionate about their chosen field. As their largest scheme BAE Systems have a range of business and engineering opportunities available, covering everything from Naval Architecture, Electrical and Software Engineering to Human Resources, Procurement and Commercial to name just a few.

For those with an interest in finance, there's the five-year, Finance Leader Development Programme (FLDP) which is a fast-track finance graduate scheme, preparing individuals to become Finance Directors of the future. The programme includes a structured and fully supported route to the highly respected Chartered Institute of Management Accountants (CIMA) qualification.

Finally, Sigma is a three year fast-track leadership programme created for people of the very highest potential. With only a few places available each year, graduates are provided with a breadth and depth of knowledge from across multiple business areas to develop as engineering and business leaders of the future.

BAE Systems also have a number of summer internship and industrial placements available in a range of business and engineering roles.

GRADUATE VACANCIES IN 2018

CONSULTING
ENGINEERING
FINANCE
GENERAL MANAGEMENT
HUMAN RESOURCES
IT
RESEARCH & DEVELOPMENT

NUMBER OF VACANCIES
350 graduate jobs

LOCATIONS OF VACANCIES

STARTING SALARY FOR 2018
£28,000-£30,000
Plus a £2,000 welcome payment.

UNIVERSITY VISITS IN 2017-18
ASTON, BATH, BIRMINGHAM, BRISTOL, CAMBRIDGE, CARDIFF, DURHAM, GLASGOW, HERIOT-WATT, IMPERIAL COLLEGE LONDON, KENT, LANCASTER, LEEDS, LIVERPOOL, LOUGHBOROUGH, MANCHESTER, NEWCASTLE, NOTTINGHAM, OXFORD, SHEFFIELD, SOUTHAMPTON, STRATHCLYDE, SURREY, UNIVERSITY COLLEGE LONDON, WARWICK, YORK
Please check with your university careers service for full details of local events.

MINIMUM ENTRY REQUIREMENTS
2.1 Degree
Relevant degree required for some roles.

APPLICATION DEADLINE
Varies by function
Please see website for full details.

FURTHER INFORMATION
www.Top100GraduateEmployers.com
Register now for the latest news, campus events, work experience and graduate vacancies at BAE Systems.

Remarkable people doing work that matters

Opportunities for graduates and undergraduates

Business
Business Development
Commercial
Human Resources
Procurement
Project Management

Engineering
Electrical & Electronic
Manufacturing & Production
Mechanical
Naval Architecture
Software
Systems

Information Technology
Cyber Security Consulting
Business Consulting
Technical Consulting
Data Analytics
Business Analytics

Finance
Financial Accounting
Management Accounting
Project Accounting

If you're ready to work on projects
that make a real difference visit:
baesystems.com/graduates

f BAE Systems Graduates
𝕏 @BAESGraduates

BAE SYSTEMS
INSPIRED WORK

Baker McKenzie.

Baker McKenzie prides itself on being the global law firm that offers a personal and professional approach to its graduates and clients alike. It's this approach that ensures the firm is ideally placed to offer graduates the best possible start to their legal career.

Baker McKenzie is a leading global law firm based in 77 offices in 47 countries and has a presence in all of the world's leading financial centres. The London office, which has been established for over 50 years, is the largest. From here over 400 lawyers serve a wide and varied network of clients, both in the UK and across the globe.

The global nature of the firm means it offers a great deal of variety to its graduates. It works hard to combine its local legal expertise with the wider experience of its international offices, providing clients with a consistent service and legal professionals the opportunity to interact with colleagues from across the world.

In terms of its client base, Baker McKenzie works principally with venture capital funds, investment banks, technology powerhouses and household name brands. Its international scope means the firm is well equipped to act on cross-border transactions and disputes. Baker McKenzie in London provides the practices that one would expect from one of the world's leading law firms, and is the recognised market leader in many of these.

The firm thrives on new talent. So it makes a significant investment in its graduates' potential through tailored training and development. Those who enjoy an intellectual challenge, are problem solvers and team players with a personable approach will feel at home at this friendly and supportive firm.

GRADUATE VACANCIES IN 2018
LAW

NUMBER OF VACANCIES
33 graduate jobs
For training contracts starting in 2020.

LOCATIONS OF VACANCIES

STARTING SALARY FOR 2018
£45,000

UNIVERSITY VISITS IN 2017-18
BELFAST, BRISTOL, CAMBRIDGE, DURHAM, EDINBURGH, EXETER, KING'S COLLEGE LONDON, LEEDS, LEICESTER, LONDON SCHOOL OF ECONOMICS, MANCHESTER, NOTTINGHAM, OXFORD, QUEEN MARY LONDON, SOUTHAMPTON, ST ANDREWS, UNIVERSITY COLLEGE LONDON, WARWICK, YORK
Please check with your university careers service for full details of local events.

MINIMUM ENTRY REQUIREMENTS
2.1 Degree

APPLICATION DEADLINE
Varies by function

FURTHER INFORMATION
www.Top100GraduateEmployers.com
Register now for the latest news, campus events, work experience and graduate vacancies at Baker McKenzie.

The impact of the Bank of England's work is uniquely far-reaching. As the country's central bank, they promote the good of the people of the UK by maintaining monetary and financial stability. The work they do, and the decisions they make, influences the daily lives of millions of people.

The Bank's primary role hasn't changed for over 300 years. But the range of work they do, and the ways in which they deliver it, is changing all the time. Today it's changing quicker than ever before. And their graduates are a key part of this progress.

Despite the nature of the Bank's work, economics is not the only way in. They welcome graduates from all degree disciplines, because quality of thinking is what counts here. Their culture is open and collaborative, where ideas are shared freely and people at every level are empowered to speak up. It is refreshingly diverse too. The Bank looks for people from all backgrounds, and individual perspectives are embraced. Successful applicants will find a wide range of societies, clubs and employee networks open to them.

Wherever they work – from Regulation, Technology and Policy Analysis to Economics and Communications – they'll take on complex work that they can be proud of. They'll tackle projects that support, shape and challenge the biggest ideas in the economy. And the work graduates do will benefit every single person in the UK.

As training is at the heart of the Bank's programme, they'll be able to grow into a real expert in their field. Equally, the support is there to explore other parts of the Bank if they wish. There are many and varied pathways available. For graduates keen to broaden their horizons, they'll have every opportunity to define their own future as the Bank itself moves forward.

GRADUATE VACANCIES IN 2018
ACCOUNTANCY
FINANCE
GENERAL MANAGEMENT
HUMAN RESOURCES
INVESTMENT BANKING
IT

NUMBER OF VACANCIES
80+ graduate jobs

LOCATIONS OF VACANCIES

STARTING SALARY FOR 2018
£30,000

UNIVERSITY VISITS IN 2017-18
ASTON, BATH, BIRMINGHAM, BRISTOL, CAMBRIDGE, CARDIFF, DURHAM, EDINBURGH, EXETER, KENT, LEEDS, LEICESTER, LONDON SCHOOL OF ECONOMICS, LOUGHBOROUGH, MANCHESTER, NOTTINGHAM, OXFORD, READING, SHEFFIELD, SURREY, WARWICK, YORK
Please check with your university careers service for full details of local events.

MINIMUM ENTRY REQUIREMENTS
2.1 Degree
300 UCAS points

APPLICATION DEADLINE
13th November 2017

FURTHER INFORMATION
www.Top100GraduateEmployers.com
Register now for the latest news, campus events, work experience and graduate vacancies at the Bank of England.

BANK OF ENGLAND

PICTURE WHAT TOMORROW'S ECONOMY COULD BE THEN GUIDE IT

We have one clear aim – to ensure stability at the heart of the UK's economy. But there are countless ways in which you could help us achieve this. From HR and Technology to Economics and Risk, you'll be encouraged and supported to follow the path that inspires you the most. And you'll enjoy real influence – not just over the projects you're involved in, but also over where your future with us goes next.

The Bank of England is changing today. **You define tomorrow.**

bankofenglandearlycareers.co.uk

Healthy economies need innovative banks to help transform and drive social progress. Barclays' ambition for bigger thinking is simple. By encouraging fresh ideas they can make a bigger difference. Interns and graduates at Barclays have many opportunities to get involved. To share big ideas. To show a better way. And to challenge what's already been done.

Barclays is a transatlantic consumer, corporate and investment bank offering products and services across personal, corporate and investment banking, credit cards and wealth management, with a strong presence in its two home markets of the UK and the US.

With over 325 years of history and expertise in banking, Barclays operates in over 40 countries and employs approximately 85,000 people. Barclays moves, lends, invests and protects money for customers and clients worldwide.

Barclays was the first bank to appoint a female bank manager, introduce ATMs, and launch credit cards and contactless payment. From the products and services they develop to the partnerships they build, they seek to improve lives and drive growth that benefits everyone.

Those joining can expect immediate responsibility. Collective challenges and inspiring collaborations will expand their minds, while ongoing training will turn fledgling ideas into groundbreaking concepts, providing the expertise that drives the bank and profession as a whole.

Barclays offers a wealth of opportunities for students from all degree disciplines. All they need is a commercial outlook, curious nature, and the ambition to help Barclays become the best bank it can be. In a positive, supportive environment, graduates will have the freedom to create smarter solutions every day.

GRADUATE VACANCIES IN 2018

FINANCE
GENERAL MANAGEMENT
HUMAN RESOURCES
INVESTMENT BANKING
IT
MARKETING
SALES

NUMBER OF VACANCIES
300+ graduate jobs

LOCATIONS OF VACANCIES

Vacancies also available in Europe, the USA, Asia and elsewhere in the world.

STARTING SALARY FOR 2018
£Competitive

UNIVERSITY VISITS IN 2017-18
BIRMINGHAM, BRISTOL, CAMBRIDGE, CARDIFF, DURHAM, EDINBURGH, EXETER, IMPERIAL COLLEGE LONDON, KING'S COLLEGE LONDON, LANCASTER, LEEDS, LEICESTER, LIVERPOOL, LONDON SCHOOL OF ECONOMICS, LOUGHBOROUGH, MANCHESTER, NEWCASTLE, NOTTINGHAM, OXFORD, SHEFFIELD, SOUTHAMPTON, SUSSEX, UNIVERSITY COLLEGE LONDON, WARWICK, YORK
Please check with your university careers service for full details of local events.

APPLICATION DEADLINE
Varies by function

FURTHER INFORMATION
www.Top100GraduateEmployers.com
Register now for the latest news, campus events, work experience and graduate vacancies at Barclays.

The latest thinking?
Time to out-think it

Barclays is a place for open minds and big ideas. It's for the openly curious, the natural collaborators, the people who believe there's always a better way.

With us, you'll have the freedom to come up with smarter solutions every day. New products to help our customers. Fresh ways to support communities. Deals that transform businesses and turn fledgling ideas into ground-breaking innovations.

It's a huge challenge, but also an incredible opportunity. The question is, are you ready to think big?

joinus.barclays

 BARCLAYS

BBC

www.bbc.co.uk/careers/trainee-schemes

twitter.com/BBCCareers

youtube.com/bbccareers   linkedin.com/company/bbc

In 1922, a Scottish engineer called John Reith was the first Director General of the BBC. He famously said he "hadn't the remotest idea as to what broadcasting was". The BBC has come a long way since then, with over 21,000 staff spread out across the world.

The BBC has nine national TV services, ten national radio stations, regional TV and Radio, online services across News, Sport, Weather, CBBC and iPlayer, international services such as the BBC World Service and World News, and its commercial arm, BBC Worldwide.

Structured entry-level trainee schemes for graduates (and also non-graduates) are available across most of the BBC's business areas; in Production, Journalism, Broadcast Engineering, Software Engineering, Research and Development, UX Design, Legal, Information Security and Communications.

The BBC's training arm, the BBC Academy, has specialists who work alongside the BBC's subject matter experts to design industry-leading training programmes; alumni from these programmes have consistently gone on to become leaders across the broadcasting sector. Competition for places is tough, with several thousand applicants routinely applying for Production and Journalism trainee programmes.

Opportunities are available across the UK, in London, Birmingham, Salford, Bristol, Cardiff, Glasgow and Belfast. Whilst academic achievement is an important entry requirement for some of the BBC's programmes, attitude, curiosity and passion are likely to impress BBC recruiters, as is a good dose of life experience and the ability to communicate and work in a team.

Recruitment takes place at various times throughout the year; the BBC's Careers website has a comprehensive list of every trainee programme and when it is open for applications. Most trainee programmes start in September.

GRADUATE VACANCIES IN 2018

ENGINEERING
GENERAL MANAGEMENT
IT
MEDIA
RESEARCH & DEVELOPMENT

NUMBER OF VACANCIES
130 graduate jobs

LOCATIONS OF VACANCIES

STARTING SALARY FOR 2018
£20,800
£25,000 in London.

UNIVERSITY VISITS IN 2017-18
ABERYSTWYTH, CARDIFF, LEEDS,
LIVERPOOL, OXFORD, YORK
Please check with your university careers service for full details of local events.

APPLICATION DEADLINE
Varies by function

FURTHER INFORMATION
www.Top100GraduateEmployers.com
Register now for the latest news, campus events, work experience and graduate vacancies at the BBC.

Be part of something special. Join the BBC
Graduate Opportunities | UK Wide | £20,800+ pa

The BBC is the world's leading public service broadcaster, known and loved internationally for its radio, television and online content.

Our aim is simple – to enrich people's lives with programmes and services that inform, educate and entertain by being the most creative organisation in the world.

Creativity is the lifeblood of our organisation. We're brave. We innovate and demonstrate creative ambition, trying new things and embracing new technology.

We're looking for the next generation of talent to keep the BBC at its very best with fresh ideas and different perspectives. The more diverse our workforce, the better able we are to respond to and reflect our audiences in all their diversity.

As a BBC graduate you will be making a difference, working on products and services that are enjoyed every day by millions of people. Our graduate schemes include journalism, software engineering, broadcast engineering, research & development, legal and production to name a few.

Be part of something special and join the BBC.

To find out more visit **www.bbc.co.uk/careers/trainee-schemes-and-apprenticeships**

The world's watching

Bloomberg

Bloomberg unleashes the power of information to inspire people who want to change the world. Well-established yet dynamic and disruptive at heart, Bloomberg is truly global, connecting influential decision-makers to a network of news, people and ideas.

It all starts with data. Anchored by the Bloomberg Professional® service (the Terminal), which offers real-time financial information to more than 325,000 subscribers globally, Bloomberg solves a variety of challenges for clients through an ever-expanding array of technology, data, news and media services that add value to information. Global Data provides the foundation for innovation as the company continues to evolve beyond traditional data analysis to provide clients with unique, meaningful and actionable information delivered through a variety of technologies and platforms.

The Enterprise Solutions business delivers the tools companies need to improve efficiency, minimise operational costs, comply with mounting regulations and achieve meaningful transparency. Bloomberg's approach helps clients not just access data, but capitalize on it in the most agile ways possible.

Bloomberg Media – digital, television, print, mobile and radio – is a critical input that reaches influential business decision makers around the world in over 150 bureaus across 73 countries. Through Bloomberg Government (BGOV), Bloomberg New Energy Finance (BNEF) and Bloomberg Bureau of National Affairs (BNA), Bloomberg provides data, news and analytics to decision makers in government, clean energy and legal markets.

Bloomberg takes care to foster a culture of community, and are dedicated to employees' well-being, offering generous benefits, training and opportunities for meaningful volunteerism.

How does
a tsunami
affect
microchip
prices?

Problem solving has always
been our first order of business.
Bringing clarity to a complex
world is our purpose.

Come find yours.
bloomberg.com/careers

Make connections **on purpose.**

Bloomberg

 **Rolls-Royce**
Motor Cars Limited

GRADUATE VACANCIES IN 2018
ENGINEERING
FINANCE
HUMAN RESOURCES
IT
LOGISTICS
MARKETING
SALES

NUMBER OF VACANCIES
20-30 graduate jobs

LOCATIONS OF VACANCIES

With its three brands BMW, MINI and Rolls-Royce Motor Cars, BMW Group is the world's leading manufacturer of premium automobiles and motorcycles, and provider of premium financial and mobility services. It operates 31 production and assembly facilities in 14 countries and has a global sales network.

As a global leader in their field, BMW Group are always looking for passionate graduates interested in developing their business experience to join their 24-month UK Graduate Programme or Global Leader Development Programme (GLDP).

The 24-month UK Graduate Programme, offered across a variety of disciplines, is a unique chance for graduates to strengthen their business profile through involvement in a range of projects and placements. Supervised by mentors and surrounded by fellow graduates, they'll gain valuable insights into business processes and strategy, as well as the opportunity to get to know BMW Group's culture and brands from the inside.

The GLDP is a unique talent development opportunity that will equip successful applicants step-by-step with the skills they need to succeed. Supported by an experienced mentor, they'll be able to benefit from this structured scheme in several ways: having the chance to work abroad, sharing know-how across borders, joining teams to tackle exciting and varied projects and building their own global network of contacts are only some of the programme's integral parts.

With the 24-month Graduate Programme and GLDP, Graduates who share BMW Group's passion for future mobility solutions, are willing to strengthen their strategic and operational competencies, and welcome the opportunity to take on new responsibilities are in good company.

STARTING SALARY FOR 2018
£31,000

UNIVERSITY VISITS IN 2017-18
ASTON, BATH, BIRMINGHAM, BRISTOL, EXETER, LOUGHBOROUGH, NOTTINGHAM TRENT, OXFORD BROOKES, PLYMOUTH, READING, SHEFFIELD, SOUTHAMPTON, SURREY, SUSSEX
Please check with your university careers service for full details of local events.

MINIMUM ENTRY REQUIREMENTS
2.1 Degree

APPLICATION DEADLINE
Year-round recruitment
Early application advised.

FURTHER INFORMATION
www.Top100GraduateEmployers.com
Register now for the latest news, campus events, work experience and graduate vacancies at BMW Group.

GET THE SKILLS TO LEAD AND SUCCEED.

THE BMW GROUP UK GRADUATE PROGRAMME AND THE GLOBAL LEADER DEVELOPMENT PROGRAMME.

Those who want to lead can learn it here, step by step, with a global leader driven by passion for innovative mobility solutions.

If you share our passion, enjoy taking on responsibilities and want to lay the foundation for a rewarding and successful career, join us on our 24-month Graduate Programme or our Global Leader Development Programme.

Apply now at www.bmwgroup.jobs/uk

www.boots.jobs/graduate-schemes

graduates@boots.co.uk

twitter.com/boots_talent 🐦 facebook.com/TalentProgrammes f

Boots is the UK's leading pharmacy-led health and beauty retailer and its purpose is to champion everyone's right to feel good. With over 2,500 stores in the UK and a heritage spanning over 165 years, Boots has a unique place in the heart of the communities it serves.

Boots is also part of a global enterprise, Walgreens Boots Alliance, which has a presence in over 25 countries. They are looking for talented, passionate graduates, who want to make a real difference, who are innovative and proactive go-getters and who can help the business grow. In return, Boots have a whole lot to offer.

The Support Office graduate programmes are based in Nottingham with opportunities in the commercial teams, HR, Global Brands and many more. All of Boots's graduates will have the chance to spend time in stores, understanding the customers, seeing how the organisation operates and working alongside fantastic store and healthcare colleagues to learn how to deliver legendary customer care.

Helping graduates to identify their strengths and preferences is very important, so Boots also offers access to a unique learning and development programme; which helps them to develop skills and knowledge that can help accelerate their career with the organisation.

Boots offer a pre-registration programme for MPharm students who can gain a true breadth and depth of experience within a community pharmacy. The programme provides the opportunity to experience delivering individual patient care as well as a range of innovative clinical services; supported by experienced tutors and pharmacist trainers.

For undergraduates, Boots also offers Year in Industry placements and Summer Internships which will provide invaluable on-the-job experience.

GRADUATE VACANCIES IN 2018

FINANCE
GENERAL MANAGEMENT
HUMAN RESOURCES
IT
LOGISTICS
MARKETING

NUMBER OF VACANCIES
30-40 graduate jobs

LOCATIONS OF VACANCIES

STARTING SALARY FOR 2018
£25,000
Plus a £1,000 welcome bonus (Support Office graduate programme only).

UNIVERSITY VISITS IN 2017-18
BIRMINGHAM, LEEDS, LEICESTER, LOUGHBOROUGH, NEWCASTLE, NOTTINGHAM, NOTTINGHAM TRENT, SHEFFIELD
Please check with your university careers service for full details of local events.

MINIMUM ENTRY REQUIREMENTS
2.1 Degree

APPLICATION DEADLINE
Varies by function

FURTHER INFORMATION
www.Top100GraduateEmployers.com
Register now for the latest news, campus events, work experience and graduate vacancies at Boots.

the bigger picture
whichever way you look at it
#boots360

www.bp.com/grads/uk

facebook.com/bpcareers **f**

linkedin.com/company/bp **in**   twitter.com/bp_careers **y**

youtube.com/BPplc **YouTube**   plus.google.com/+bp **G+**

BP develops and produces energy resources that benefit people across the world. Constantly pushing the boundaries of what's achievable, they rely on their vast team of talented individuals to come together and make it possible. Together, their future has no limits.

Geoscientists sending sound waves through the earth to find new oil and gas reserves. Engineers building platforms in the ocean for extraction. Traders anticipating and reacting to changes in the markets. BP take on graduates and interns at every stage of the energy life cycle. So whichever route a student or graduate chooses, they'll be starting a career path that can really take them places.

Whether applicants want to be a business leader, a world-class scientist or a ground-breaking engineer, BP have a programme to suit. For graduates, their 2-3 year 'Challenge' and supply and trading programmes will provide the skills and experience they need to succeed – whatever field they're in. For penultimate-year undergraduates and postgraduates, they offer paid internships that last for a full 12 months or for 11 weeks over the summer months – providing a chance to gain valuable insights into how BP works as a business.

It's possible to learn a lot as a BP graduate or intern. But most important of all, it's the start of a career path that can really take them places. At BP, it's about more than just academic achievements. Their approach is built on teamwork and respect, inclusion and ambition. It's this approach that enables them to deliver excellent energy safely. And it's these values that graduates will share.

To understand what life as a BP graduate or intern is really like, hear from the people who live it. Visit their careers site to get graduate perspectives on the things that matter. Or, to find the right role, use BP's online degree matcher tool – find it at bp.com/degreematcher.

GRADUATE VACANCIES IN 2018

ACCOUNTANCY

ENGINEERING

FINANCE

HUMAN RESOURCES

IT

LOGISTICS

PURCHASING

RESEARCH & DEVELOPMENT

RETAILING

SALES

NUMBER OF VACANCIES
100+ graduate jobs

LOCATIONS OF VACANCIES

STARTING SALARY FOR 2018
£33,000+
Plus a £3,000 settling-in allowance.

UNIVERSITY VISITS IN 2017-18
ABERDEEN, BATH, BIRMINGHAM, CAMBRIDGE, DURHAM, HERIOT-WATT, IMPERIAL COLLEGE LONDON, LONDON SCHOOL OF ECONOMICS, MANCHESTER, NOTTINGHAM, OXFORD, SHEFFIELD, STRATHCLYDE, UNIVERSITY COLLEGE LONDON
Please check with your university careers service for full details of local events.

MINIMUM ENTRY REQUIREMENTS
2.1 Degree

APPLICATION DEADLINE
Varies by function

FURTHER INFORMATION
www.Top100GraduateEmployers.com
Register now for the latest news, campus events, work experience and graduate vacancies at BP.

"Taking on responsibility and owning projects is really exciting."

LeAnn's perspective on opportunity

Intern and graduate opportunities

From creating world-class products to developing secure, sustainable energy for the future, there's more to BP than you might think. As a graduate, you'll make a difference from day one, embarking on a real career with real responsibilities. So from business and trading, to engineering and science, whatever it is you're doing, you'll be playing your part in our success.

To find out more visit bp.com/grads/uk

bp

facebook.com/BTEarlyCareers **f**

linkedin.com/company/BT **in**   twitter.com/BTearlycareers **y**

GRADUATE VACANCIES IN 2018

GENERAL MANAGEMENT
HUMAN RESOURCES
IT
LAW
LOGISTICS
MARKETING
PURCHASING
RESEARCH & DEVELOPMENT
SALES

NUMBER OF VACANCIES
250+ graduate jobs

LOCATIONS OF VACANCIES

STARTING SALARY FOR 2018
£28,250+

UNIVERSITY VISITS IN 2017-18
BATH, BELFAST, BIRMINGHAM, BRISTOL,
CAMBRIDGE, CARDIFF, DURHAM,
EAST ANGLIA, ESSEX, EXETER, KENT,
LANCASTER, LEICESTER, LOUGHBOROUGH,
NOTTINGHAM, QUEEN MARY LONDON,
SHEFFIELD, SOUTHAMPTON,
STRATHCLYDE, ULSTER, UNIVERSITY
COLLEGE LONDON, WARWICK
Please check with your university careers
service for full details of local events.

MINIMUM ENTRY REQUIREMENTS
2.1 Degree

APPLICATION DEADLINE
Varies by function

FURTHER INFORMATION
www.Top100GraduateEmployers.com
Register now for the latest news, campus
events, work experience and graduate
vacancies at BT.

Every day BT's people touch the lives of millions, providing services that help customers get the most out of their working and personal lives. That's a privilege and a responsibility. At BT, they use the power of communications to make a better world. Helping people, businesses and communities create possibilities.

BT is one of the world's leading providers of communications services and solutions, with customers in 180 countries. They operate globally and deliver locally. BT's unique breadth of scope, reach and capability helps solve the most complex business communications requirements on a global scale. They're innovative in their thinking and dependable in their delivery.

BT have a proven track record in inventions that change the world. But, ground-breaking innovations don't just happen – it takes drive, passion and a thirst for knowledge and solutions in every area of BT.

Diversity is at the very heart of the company. In order to provide the very best products and services to a varied customer base they need a diverse workforce to imagine, create and deliver the solutions required both now and into the future. This means creating and maintaining a working environment that includes and values diversity.

BT's graduates are personable, straightforward and brilliant. BT looks for all of these qualities. And more. They look for people who don't wait to be told what to do, and who can't wait to get involved. BT's graduate programme focuses on developing the talented specialists and leaders of the future. Successful applicants get all the training and development they need to create meaningful and successful careers across the world of business and technology.

LET'S CREATE THE FUTURE

Life today is built on connectivity. As a global innovations company, we use the power of communications to make a better world.

From broadband and TV to mobile, we're driven by the exhilaration of building an ever-growing range of services that help our customers get more out of life. But there's so much more to BT than that. Our research and development teams help vehicle manufactures make smarter cars, let consultants treat patients remotely and provide secure finger print technology for festival goers.

Our history is all about shaping the future with ground breaking ideas. Today, we're proud to be the UK's number one tech sector investor in R&D, with 14,000 scientists and technologists leading innovation in BT. If you share our passion for putting customers at the heart of what we do, we'll invest in your future too.

www.btplc.com/Careercentre/earlycareers

graduates.cancerresearchuk.org

graduate@cancer.org.uk

Cancer. Be afraid. CRUK is a world-leading organisation funding science through exceptional fundraising efforts, raising £520m last year. Its ambition is to see 3/4 of people surviving within the next 20 years – focusing on prevention, early diagnosis, and development and personalising treatments to be more effective.

Graduates who join CRUK do something different, something extraordinary. They're changing lives. CRUK are looking for smart, sharp minded graduates to help achieve their goals. Their graduates are passionate in their work, determined, stand out communicators and effective relationship builders.

What does a graduate scheme at an organisation like this offer? All graduates are put through their paces from the very beginning. Whether joining Fundraising & Marketing; Scientific Strategy and Funding; Project Management & Digital; Finance, HR or Policy, Information and Communications streams, they will have the exciting opportunity to rotate across four diverse business areas over the course of two years.

Graduates receive support and challenge from senior mentors, peers and placement managers along their journey with formal training whilst transitioning between placements. Placements are varied, stretching and business critical. From day one, graduates will be working on high profile projects with leaders across the organisation; drawing on and developing their individual strengths, talents and experience. CRUK invests in their talent, therefore all of their graduate placements are permanent roles.

As well as graduate opportunities, Cancer Research UK offers a vast array of entry level jobs for recent graduates, sandwich placements and volunteering opportunities including award winning twelve week internships.

CRUK wants like minds, and the best minds, to help beat cancer sooner.

GRADUATE VACANCIES IN 2018
ACCOUNTANCY
FINANCE
HUMAN RESOURCES
IT
MARKETING
RESEARCH & DEVELOPMENT

NUMBER OF VACANCIES
10 graduate jobs

LOCATIONS OF VACANCIES

STARTING SALARY FOR 2018
£25,000

UNIVERSITY VISITS IN 2017-18
ASTON, BATH, BIRMINGHAM, BRISTOL, BRUNEL, CAMBRIDGE, CARDIFF, CITY, DURHAM, EAST ANGLIA, EDINBURGH, ESSEX, EXETER, GLASGOW, IMPERIAL COLLEGE LONDON, KING'S COLLEGE LONDON, LEEDS, LEICESTER, LIVERPOOL, MANCHESTER, NEWCASTLE, NOTTINGHAM, OXFORD, OXFORD BROOKES, SHEFFIELD
Please check with your university careers service for full details of local events.

MINIMUM ENTRY REQUIREMENTS
2.1 Degree

APPLICATION DEADLINE
Late November 2017

FURTHER INFORMATION
www.Top100GraduateEmployers.com
Register now for the latest news, campus events, work experience and graduate vacancies at Cancer Research UK.

AMBITIOUS
SMART ~~FAST-PACED~~ INSPIRING
DRIVING ~~SHARP~~
CHANGE
UNITED
~~PIONEERING~~
VERSATILE CHALLENGING
~~LIFE-SAVING~~ PERCEPTIONS

THIS IS HOW IT FEELS HELPING TO BEAT CANCER.
For your chance to experience it, go to cruk.org/graduates

CANCER
RESEARCH
UK

centrica

centrica

Centrica plc is an international energy and services company with around 27 million customer accounts and a worldwide workforce of over 36,000 employees. It operates mainly in the UK, Ireland and North America through strong brands such as British Gas, Bord Gáis and Direct Energy.

Centrica is a top 50 FTSE 100 company focused on satisfying the changing needs of its customers by delivering high levels of customer service, and improving customer engagement and loyalty. It is developing innovative products through its Hive brand, as well as offers and solutions underpinned by an investment in technology.

Centrica gives graduates from a broad range of degree disciplines the opportunity to work right across the company in Connected Home, Energy Supply & Services, Distributed Energy & Power and Energy Marketing & Trading. The graduate programme has been designed to offer a comprehensive grounding in the business; those who are ambitious and commercially savvy have an outstanding opportunity to make a big impact within this diverse organisation.

Developing and investing in graduates is important to Centrica. Graduate talent boards ensure graduates have the opportunity to fulfill their potential and are equipped with the right skills and behaviours to help grow the business by implementing – and one day helping shape – Centrica's strategy. Centrica's programme offers graduates who are excited by big challenges the opportunity to get involved in a variety of business areas, as well as receiving support and rewards along the way.

Centrica also offer a ten-week summer placement programme. It is a great opportunity to gain valuable work experience but also students could secure a graduate role for the following year's intake.

GRADUATE VACANCIES IN 2018

ENGINEERING
FINANCE
GENERAL MANAGEMENT
HUMAN RESOURCES
IT
MARKETING
PURCHASING
SALES

NUMBER OF VACANCIES
50+ graduate jobs

LOCATIONS OF VACANCIES

STARTING SALARY FOR 2018
£27,000-£38,000
Plus a £3,000 joining bonus, performance-related bonuses and flexible benefits.

UNIVERSITY VISITS IN 2017-18
ABERDEEN, BATH, BIRMINGHAM, BRISTOL, BRUNEL, CAMBRIDGE, CARDIFF, DURHAM, EDINBURGH, EXETER, IMPERIAL COLLEGE LONDON, KING'S COLLEGE LONDON, LANCASTER, LEEDS, LEICESTER, LIVERPOOL, LONDON SCHOOL OF ECONOMICS, LOUGHBOROUGH, MANCHESTER, NEWCASTLE, NOTTINGHAM, OXFORD, READING, ROYAL HOLLOWAY, SHEFFIELD, SOUTHAMPTON, STRATHCLYDE, SWANSEA, UNIVERSITY COLLEGE LONDON, WARWICK, YORK
Please check with your university careers service for full details of local events.

MINIMUM ENTRY REQUIREMENTS
2.1 Degree

APPLICATION DEADLINE
21st November 2017

FURTHER INFORMATION
www.Top100GraduateEmployers.com
Register now for the latest news, campus events, work experience and graduate vacancies at Centrica.

life @ centrica

ME!

#summeratcentrica

SEARCH FOR US

Centrica Graduate Scheme

mer Placement

STAFF PASS

Joanne Bailey
Centrica Graduate Scheme

centrica

Like what you see? With so many new experiences and challenges, you'll find that life at Centrica is never dull. If you've got the talent and ambition, then we've got the tools and development programmes to help you achieve your potential.

From roles involving hard hats to those more suited to laptops, you'll find that each of our graduate programmes comes loaded with everything you need to build a successful and rewarding career. As the UK's leading energy supplier, we can offer you more than most when choosing a graduate programme. With opportunities in a variety of business areas that each look for a different type of graduate, you're bound to find something to suit you – whatever you're currently studying or whatever you'd like to do. We even run a 10-week Summer Placement programme too, perfect if you're looking to gain experience with a company at the top of its game.

To find out more search #summeratcentrica
Find us on Facebook @CentricaCareers
Or visit www.centrica.com/graduates

 Bord Gáis Energy
 British Gas
 Direct Energy
 DYNO
HIVE
Local Heroes

charity works •••••
careers that make a difference

www.charity-works.co.uk

info@charity-works.co.uk ✉

twitter.com/charityworksUK 🐦   facebook.com/charityworksuk **f**

instagram.com/charityworksuk 📷   linkedin.com/company/charityworks **in**

Charityworks is the UK non-profit sector's graduate scheme, recruiting around 150 graduates each year. It's a 12-month, paid full-time job in a partner charity or housing association and an acclaimed leadership programme that introduces graduates to what they need to work and lead in the non-profit sector.

In a placement, graduates could be providing vital business support and evaluation at a national charity like NSPCC, leading on the improvement of infrastructure projects with a leading housing charity, driving international business with the RNLI, or serving a community in a local project. Wherever they're placed, they'll have a chance to make a real impact through their work.

Alongside the placement, graduates will take part in a leadership development programme. They'll be matched with a Charityworks Programme Manager and external mentor to help them make the most of the year. Twice a month they'll come together with their fellow trainees and leaders across the sector to explore and debate the key issues affecting their work and society as a whole. Graduates will also produce their own research, helping to raise their profile and develop their understanding of their environment.

At the end of the 12-month scheme they will have the experience and skills to kick-start a professional career in the UK non-profit sector and beyond. Charityworks graduates are highly desired, with 98% securing employment within three months if they were looking for it. Typically, over 66% of graduates stay in their host organisations at the end of the year, and 96% of graduates since 2009 have remained within the non-profit or public sector – some have even gone on to start their own organisations.

Whatever graduates want to do in the long-term, Charityworks is a fantastic way to launch their career and change the world for a living.

GRADUATE VACANCIES IN 2018

FINANCE
GENERAL MANAGEMENT
HUMAN RESOURCES
IT
MARKETING
MEDIA
RESEARCH & DEVELOPMENT

NUMBER OF VACANCIES
150 graduate jobs

LOCATIONS OF VACANCIES

STARTING SALARY FOR 2018
£18,000-£20,000

UNIVERSITY VISITS IN 2017-18
ABERDEEN, BATH, BIRMINGHAM, BRISTOL, BRUNEL, CAMBRIDGE, CARDIFF, CITY, DUNDEE, DURHAM, EAST ANGLIA, EDINBURGH, EXETER, GLASGOW, HERIOT-WATT, HULL, IMPERIAL COLLEGE LONDON, KING'S COLLEGE LONDON, LANCASTER, LEEDS, LEICESTER, LIVERPOOL, LONDON SCHOOL OF ECONOMICS, LOUGHBOROUGH, MANCHESTER, NEWCASTLE, NORTHUMBRIA, NOTTINGHAM, OXFORD, QUEEN MARY LONDON, READING, SCHOOL OF AFRICAN STUDIES, SHEFFIELD, SOUTHAMPTON, ST ANDREWS, SURREY, SUSSEX, UNIVERSITY COLLEGE LONDON, WARWICK, YORK
Please check with your university careers service for full details of local events.

MINIMUM ENTRY REQUIREMENTS
2.1 Degree

APPLICATION DEADLINE
28th February 2018

FURTHER INFORMATION
www.Top100GraduateEmployers.com
Register now for the latest news, campus events, work experience and graduate vacancies at Charityworks.

POVERTY.
AFFORDABLE HOUSING.
DOMESTIC VIOLENCE.
CLIMATE CHANGE.
SOCIAL CARE.

WHAT ROLE WILL YOU PLAY?

Charityworks.
Change the world
for a living.

Charityworks; Registered Charity No. 1136964, Company No. 7304744

Civil Service
Fast Stream

www.faststream.gov.uk

faststream@parity.net ✉

twitter.com/faststreamuk 🐦 facebook.com/faststream f

youtube.com/theFaststreamuk ▶️ linkedin.com/company/civil-service-fast-stream in

Working at the heart of government, Fast Streamers work on some of the most complex issues facing Britain and the rest of the world. With 16 different schemes, there are a diversity of roles, each offering the opportunity to forge a brilliant career and benefit from high-quality professional development.

The Fast Stream is a structured, accelerated learning and development programme for those who have the motivation and potential to become future leaders of the Civil Service. Fast Streamers are given considerable responsibility from the outset: they are stretched and challenged on a daily basis, they move between posts to gain a wide range of contrasting experiences and build up an impressive portfolio of skills and knowledge.

There are opportunities available across the UK and across professions including: digital, communications, policy development, corporate services, people management, commercial awareness, financial management and project management, giving Fast Streamers a wide understanding of how government delivers public services.

The Civil Service is a great place to work, where staff are truly valued. Fast Streamers have great work-life balance and a career that enables them to give something back. The Civil Service is united by a strong sense of public service. Enduring values are integrity, honesty, impartiality and objectivity, these run through all that it does.

Society is best served by a Civil Service which is as diverse as itself. There's no such thing as a typical Fast Streamer, and graduates from a wide range of backgrounds are excited by the idea of making a positive and highly visible impact on the most important and exciting issues facing the country.

There's no limit to where a Fast Stream career in the Civil Service can lead.

GRADUATE VACANCIES IN 2018
FINANCE
GENERAL MANAGEMENT
HUMAN RESOURCES
IT
MARKETING
PURCHASING
RESEARCH & DEVELOPMENT

NUMBER OF VACANCIES
1,000 graduate jobs

LOCATIONS OF VACANCIES

STARTING SALARY FOR 2018
£25,000-£28,000

UNIVERSITY VISITS IN 2017-18
ABERYSTWYTH, ASTON, BELFAST, BIRMINGHAM, BRADFORD, BRISTOL, BRUNEL, CARDIFF, CITY, DURHAM, EAST ANGLIA, EDINBURGH, ESSEX, EXETER, GLASGOW, HULL, KING'S COLLEGE LONDON, KENT, LANCASTER, LEEDS, LEICESTER, LIVERPOOL, LONDON SCHOOL OF ECONOMICS, MANCHESTER, NEWCASTLE, NORTHUMBRIA, NOTTINGHAM, NOTTINGHAM TRENT, QUEEN MARY LONDON, READING, ROYAL HOLLOWAY, SCHOOL OF AFRICAN STUDIES, SHEFFIELD, SOUTHAMPTON, SUSSEX, UNIVERSITY COLLEGE LONDON, WARWICK, YORK
Please check with your university careers service for full details of local events.

MINIMUM ENTRY REQUIREMENTS
2.2 Degree

APPLICATION DEADLINE
Late October 2017

FURTHER INFORMATION
www.Top100GraduateEmployers.com
Register now for the latest news, campus events, work experience and graduate vacancies at the Civil Service Fast Stream.

Where talented people do brilliant things

The Civil Service Fast Stream is looking for visionaries, creative thinkers, agile minds and talented problem solvers. People from all kinds of backgrounds, with the imagination to see things not just as they are, but how they could be.

We're searching for people who are able to flex and adapt to a limitless range of situations. Innovative people who want to be challenged. Those with the intellect and the emotional intelligence to motivate and inspire. People who want to make a real difference in the world.

Whatever your talent, Fast Stream offers a dynamic career path, with a variety of graduate opportunities available across the UK.

You'll benefit from a structured programme, high-quality learning, a supportive environment and a range of professional and social peer networks, to help you fulfil your potential.

If you're a pioneer, a trailblazer, innovator or future leader, you could be one of the 1000+ talented people who will join us in 2018.

Start your application today at www.faststream.gov.uk

Voted Best Public Sector Graduate Employer 2017

Civil Service Fast Stream   Where will you lead?

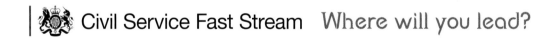

Law . Tax

www.cms.law
facebook.com/CMSUKGraduates
instagram.com/CMSGraduates
twitter.com/CMSUK_Graduates

GRADUATE VACANCIES IN 2018
LAW

NUMBER OF VACANCIES
65 graduate jobs
For training contracts starting in 2020.

LOCATIONS OF VACANCIES

With 71 offices in over 40 countries, CMS is a global elite law firm. In 2017, CMS UK, Nabarro LLP and Olswang LLP combined in what was the largest ever merger in the UK legal industry. The new combined firm, CMS, is now the 6th largest in the UK by revenue and the 6th largest globally by headcount.

CMS is a new kind of future-facing law firm. By combining top quality sector expertise with international scale and a strategy to become a progressive technology-driven firm, CMS delivers excellence for its clients and is committed to ensuring all employees achieve their full potential.

Across its six core sectors of Energy, Financial Services, Infrastructure and Project Finance, Lifesciences and Healthcare, Real Estate and Technology, Media and Communications, CMS has some of the brightest and most creative legal minds. Its lawyers are immersed in the clients' worlds, are genuine experts in their fields and knowledgeable about the issues that lie ahead.

The firm is modern and ambitious: employing more than 5,500 fee earners worldwide it creates strong relationships with clients and staff, meaning it is looking for lawyers with excellent personal skills as well as being technically strong. In return, CMS offers world-class training and development opportunities.

The CMS Academy is CMS's next generation vacation scheme starting with one week 'business of law' training in London. This comprises panel discussions with clients, case studies, work simulation exercises and client visits amongst other things! It is an intense but fully rewarding week where students will experience first-hand the commitment from the firm to make them the best lawyer for the future. The second part of the programme includes a two-week internship within one of their UK offices where participants gain real experience in a commercial environment and develop skills needed to succeed as a trainee solicitor.

STARTING SALARY FOR 2018
£26,000-£40,000

UNIVERSITY VISITS IN 2017-18
BRISTOL, CAMBRIDGE, DUNDEE, EDINBURGH, EXETER, GLASGOW, KING'S COLLEGE LONDON, LONDON SCHOOL OF ECONOMICS, MANCHESTER, NOTTINGHAM, SHEFFIELD, STRATHCLYDE, UNIVERSITY COLLEGE LONDON, WARWICK
Please check with your university careers service for full details of local events.

MINIMUM ENTRY REQUIREMENTS
2.1 Degree

APPLICATION DEADLINE
Please see website for full details.

FURTHER INFORMATION
www.Top100GraduateEmployers.com
Register now for the latest news, campus events, work experience and graduate vacancies at CMS.

DANONE

PRODUCTS AND SERVICES
FOR EVERY STAGE OF LIFE.

For over 100 years, a unique purpose to 'bring health through food and beverages to as many people as possible', has inspired world leading brands such as Evian, Activia, Cow&Gate and Nutricia. Today, this purpose unites 100,000 Danone employees behind products that reach nine million consumers worldwide.

The UK Danone graduate scheme is designed for motivated individuals who are passionate about Danone's mission and values. In return, Danone provides them with the essential skills and behaviours needed to grow into committed and inspirational leaders.

Although a global business, Danone has a non-hierarchical structure that ensures every employee is equally valued, respected and empowered to make a difference. For graduates, that means they are placed in influential roles, with independence and autonomy, gaining extensive experience to support their personal progression. Graduates will be at the cutting edge of the business, playing a key role from the start.

Individual growth and development are an integral part of the company's DNA. A graduate's learning journey is completely personalised, based on their career aspirations and developmental targets. Along the way, they are fully supported by an internal coach and a network of key individuals who are committed to helping them achieve their goals.

Danone was built on the pioneering spirit of its founders. It's their spirit that underpins the core values of the entire organisation and their legacy is the development of a business that began and remains at the forefront of innovation. In its graduates, Danone is looking for new and exciting visionaries to continue this legacy and to contribute to a healthier world.

GRADUATE VACANCIES IN 2018

MARKETING

SALES

NUMBER OF VACANCIES
10-20 graduate jobs

LOCATIONS OF VACANCIES

STARTING SALARY FOR 2018
£29,500
Plus a 3-6% bonus and flexible benefits.

UNIVERSITY VISITS IN 2017-18
ASTON, BATH, BIRMINGHAM, BRISTOL, DURHAM, EXETER, KING'S COLLEGE LONDON, LANCASTER, NOTTINGHAM, WARWICK
Please check with your university careers service for full details of local events.

MINIMUM ENTRY REQUIREMENTS
2.1 Degree
300-320 UCAS points
Dependent on role.
Relevant degree required for some roles.

APPLICATION DEADLINE
31st October 2017

FURTHER INFORMATION
www.Top100GraduateEmployers.com
*Register now for the latest news, campus events, work experience and graduate vacancies at **Danone**.*

OUR SALES OF WATER GENERATES
€4.7 BILLION...
#CHALLENGETODAY
Join Danone and help us to continue our mission to bring health through food.
Applications now open.
evian
EAU MINERALE NATURELLE
NATURAL MINERAL WATER
50 cL
#HEALTHIERTOMMOROW
...BUT WE NEVER TAKE MORE THAN NATURE OFFERS*
*Danone ensures reasoned use of every water source, under the control of hydro-geologists, so that the sources continue to replenish themselves at a natural rate. The amount drawn respects the resource, which is replenished by nature year after year.
Challenge today for a healthier tomorrow
DANONE
danone.co.uk/graduates

studentrecruitment@deloitte.co.uk ✉

twitter.com/deloittecareers 𝕏   facebook.com/deloittecareersuk **f**

instagram.com/deloittecareersuk 📷   youtube.com/DeloitteCareersUK ▶

Deloitte.

GRADUATE VACANCIES IN 2018

ACCOUNTANCY

CONSULTING

ENGINEERING

FINANCE

IT

NUMBER OF VACANCIES
900 graduate jobs

LOCATIONS OF VACANCIES

A career, full of challenges, learning, qualifications and progression. Graduates will find it all at Deloitte – and more. From Human Capital to Tax Consulting, Audit and Finance to Cyber and Digital, Deloitte is reshaping both the business and technology landscape.

In this ever more complex world, it's the smartest and most caring people that make the difference, because they're driven by imagination and the desire to add value. They dream bigger, think creatively and deliver real impact.

Deloitte is among the very few firms where intellect is integrated with action. Upholding the integrity of organisations, delivering end-to-end improvement programmes, and turning disruption into opportunity. At Deloitte, graduates discover a place where everyone is empowered to share ideas and make things happen – for clients, colleagues and society.

Because that's what they do. Supporting enterprises, in collaboration with Apple, to change the way they work. With McLaren Applied Technologies, building data-driven business products with artificial intelligence. Improving traffic and accident response times. Raising quality in supply chains. And engineering live monitoring and treatment in healthcare. They're redesigning the art of Audit and Tax by forecasting the future, automating tasks and dedicating people to problem solving.

Imagine building a professional career, gaining recognised qualifications and developing in a place where everyone connects and collaborates, across the world. Where every individual has a voice, respect is the mindset, agile working is the norm, and all are encouraged to challenge. Deloitte's success is all due to its people. People who are curious, imaginative and unafraid to stand out. People who are making an impact together.

STARTING SALARY FOR 2018
£Competitive

UNIVERSITY VISITS IN 2017-18
ABERDEEN, ASTON, BATH, BELFAST, BIRMINGHAM, BRISTOL, BRUNEL, CAMBRIDGE, CARDIFF, DURHAM, EAST ANGLIA, EDINBURGH, EXETER, GLASGOW, IMPERIAL COLLEGE LONDON, KING'S COLLEGE LONDON, KENT, LANCASTER, LEEDS, LEICESTER, LIVERPOOL, LONDON SCHOOL OF ECONOMICS, LOUGHBOROUGH, MANCHESTER, NEWCASTLE, NOTTINGHAM, NOTTINGHAM TRENT, OXFORD, QUEEN MARY LONDON, READING, ROYAL HOLLOWAY, SHEFFIELD, SOUTHAMPTON, ST ANDREWS, STRATHCLYDE, SURREY, SUSSEX, ULSTER, UNIVERSITY COLLEGE LONDON, WARWICK, YORK
Please check with your university careers service for full details of local events.

MINIMUM ENTRY REQUIREMENTS
2.1 Degree
Relevant degree required for some roles.

APPLICATION DEADLINE
October/November 2017
Early application advised.

FURTHER INFORMATION
www.Top100GraduateEmployers.com
Register now for the latest news, campus events, work experience and graduate vacancies at Deloitte.

Deloitte.

For the curious.

We believe there is only one way to reinvent the way we work: turn our imagination into action, challenge the old and influence the new.

Here's to us, to the curious, the open minded, the doers. Those who can inspire leaders and pioneer new solutions. Those who are not afraid to stand out and make unexpected things happen. Together.

What impact will you make?

deloitte.co.uk/graduates

db.com/careers

twitter.com/careersDB
youtube.com/deutschebankgroup
facebook.com/DeutscheBankCareers
linkedin.com/company/deutsche-bank/careers

Deutsche Bank provides commercial and investment banking, retail banking, transaction banking and asset and wealth management products and services to corporations, governments, institutional investors, small and medium-sized businesses, and private individuals.

At Deutsche Bank, original thinkers are given the space and training needed to excel. Innovators by nature will find a place where they can unleash their potential. As Germany's leading bank, with a strong position in Europe and a significant presence in the Americas and Asia Pacific, Deutsche Bank recruits interns and graduates from a broad range of backgrounds for a wide variety of roles.

Graduates won't necessarily need a financial or mathematical background – although there are some roles where strong numerical skills are needed. No matter the background, the bank is looking for students who are full of imagination, enjoy solving problems and respond positively to complex challenges, where they can discover a career to look forward to at Deutsche Bank.

Wherever a student's interest lies – in investment banking, trading, technology, human resources, risk management or another of the bank's many business areas – they'll discover resources, training and opportunities designed to keep them ahead of the curve. At Deutsche Bank, graduates work alongside senior leaders, on projects that have a positive impact for their clients, and enjoy global exposure from day one. Brilliant thinking is put into action.

Graduates who are full of imagination, enjoy solving problems and respond positively to complex challenges, will discover a career to look forward to at Deutsche Bank.

When you make an impact on our business

The feeling you get when you put a great idea into action is an exciting part of developing your career. That's why, at Deutsche Bank, we give brilliant thoughts, and thinkers, the room and tools they need to work. Here, you'll think and speak freely, developing your career, plans and skills in a direction you believe in. And, with a combination of world-class training and stimulating challenges, there's a lot for you to choose from.

Grow your potential. Make an impact. Discover a career to look forward to at db.com/careers

DLA PIPER

www.dlapipergraduates.com/uk

facebook.com/DLAPiperGlobal [f] recruitment_graduate@dlapiper.com [✉]
linkedin.com/company/dla-piper-uk-graduates [in] twitter.com/DLA_Piper_Grads [✔]

DLA Piper is a global law firm with lawyers located in more than 40 countries throughout the Americas, Europe, the Middle East, Africa and Asia Pacific, positioning it to help clients with their legal needs around the world. In the UK, it provides legal advice from London and the other major centres.

Unlike many law firms, DLA Piper is organised to provide clients with a range of essential business advice, not just on large scale mergers and acquisitions and banking deals but also on people and employment, commercial dealings, litigation, insurance, real estate, IT, intellectual property, plans for restructuring and tax. It has a comprehensive, award-winning client relationship management programme and the brand is built upon local legal excellence and global capability.

DLA Piper looks for opportunities to use its strength as a leading business law firm to make a positive contribution in their local and global communities. The firm's Responsible Business initiatives demonstrate how their values are embedded in the way the firm engages with its people, its clients and its communities.

Within its trainee cohort the firm needs a diverse group of highly talented individuals who are naturally inquisitive, have plenty of drive, and who show a genuine commitment to developing a career as a lawyer. In return, DLA Piper offers an ambitious and innovative environment in which people can build a dynamic, successful and international career.

Trainees complete four six-month seats and are given an opportunity to express what areas of law they would like to experience during their training contracts. They have the opportunity to do a seat abroad, or a client secondment.

GRADUATE VACANCIES IN 2018
LAW

NUMBER OF VACANCIES
70 graduate jobs
For training contracts starting in 2020.

LOCATIONS OF VACANCIES

Vacancies also available in Europe, the USA and Asia.

STARTING SALARY FOR 2018
£27,000-£44,000

UNIVERSITY VISITS IN 2017-18
ABERDEEN, ASTON, BATH, BIRMINGHAM, BRISTOL, CAMBRIDGE, CITY, DURHAM, EDINBURGH, EXETER, GLASGOW, IMPERIAL COLLEGE LONDON, KING'S COLLEGE LONDON, LANCASTER, LEEDS, LEICESTER, LIVERPOOL, LONDON SCHOOL OF ECONOMICS, LOUGHBOROUGH, MANCHESTER, NEWCASTLE, NOTTINGHAM, OXFORD, READING, SHEFFIELD, SOUTHAMPTON, ST ANDREWS, UNIVERSITY COLLEGE LONDON, WARWICK, YORK
Please check with your university careers service for full details of local events.

MINIMUM ENTRY REQUIREMENTS
2.1 Degree

APPLICATION DEADLINE
Varies by function

FURTHER INFORMATION
www.Top100GraduateEmployers.com
*Register now for the latest news, campus events, work experience and graduate vacancies at **DLA Piper**.*

110 TOP 100 GRADUATE EMPLOYERS

BIGGER

OPPORTUNITIES

· ·

DLA Piper offers big opportunities to ambitious graduates – big firm, big clients, big careers.

Don't just take our word for it. Find out more at www.dlapipergraduates.co.uk

dyson

Dyson is a global technology enterprise. They transform every category they enter with iconic re-inventions that simply work better. Dyson people apply 'wrong thinking', experiment without fear and create machines that defy convention. The future is bright and the next few years will be their busiest yet.

For 25 years, Dyson has been looking beyond the existing solutions to invent new technology. A hand dryer that doesn't use heat. A fan with no blades. An intelligent robot, capable of cleaning properly first time around. The hair dryer, re-thought. All work better. All pioneer. All are unique.

Dyson is now going through its largest expansion to date as their £2.5 billion investment in future technology continues. Earlier this year saw the opening of new Technology Centres in Singapore and Shanghai – housing the latest development labs, bringing together hardware and software expertise. Dyson has doubled the size of their research and design HQ in Wiltshire and with plans underway to build a second campus, just five miles from Dyson HQ, their UK footprint will increase tenfold. With this brings graduate opportunities that are bigger, more global, more diverse and more disruptive than ever.

But they don't just recruit engineers – there's a lot going on outside the labs too. From marketing, to finance, to software, Dyson have an underlying desire to make things work better. And their graduates learn their trade, not by shadowing, but by being in the spotlight. It's an approach that brings out the best in their new talent – turning them from first-timers into major achievers.

They want intelligent, articulate minds with the right attitude. People with a passion for technology. People who go beyond the job description. People who demonstrate the same qualities that drove James Dyson on through 5,127 prototypes and rejections – perseverance, perfectionism and wrong thinking.

GRADUATE VACANCIES IN 2018
ACCOUNTANCY
ENGINEERING
FINANCE
HUMAN RESOURCES
IT
LOGISTICS
MARKETING
MEDIA
SALES

NUMBER OF VACANCIES
100 graduate jobs

LOCATIONS OF VACANCIES

STARTING SALARY FOR 2018
£26,500
Plus a £2,000 sign-on bonus.

UNIVERSITY VISITS IN 2017-18
BATH, BRISTOL, CAMBRIDGE, EDINBURGH, EXETER, IMPERIAL COLLEGE LONDON, KING'S COLLEGE LONDON, LEEDS, LOUGHBOROUGH, MANCHESTER, NEWCASTLE, OXFORD, SHEFFIELD, SOUTHAMPTON, UNIVERSITY COLLEGE LONDON, WARWICK
Please check with your university careers service for full details of local events.

MINIMUM ENTRY REQUIREMENTS
2.1 Degree
Relevant degree required for some roles.

APPLICATION DEADLINE
Varies by function

FURTHER INFORMATION
www.Top100GraduateEmployers.com
*Register now for the latest news, campus events, work experience and graduate vacancies at **Dyson**.*

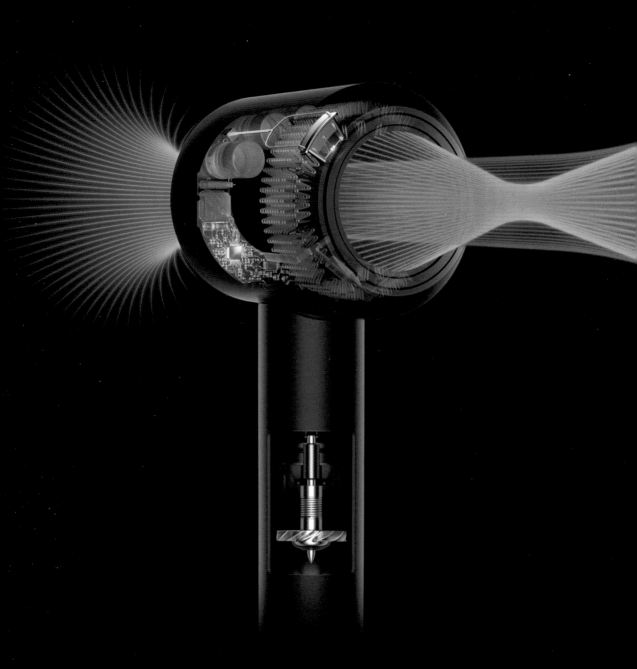

Re-think the rules.

We're looking for the best and brightest graduates to shape
our future. There's nothing conventional about a Dyson career,
so only the most ambitious need apply. At the forefront of our
global business, you won't just learn how things are done –
you'll find ways to make them better.

careers.dyson.com/early-careers

ExxonMobil

Global fundamentals

Consider how modern energy enriches your life. Now consider the 7 billion other people on earth who also use energy each day to make their own lives richer, more productive, safer and healthier. Then you will recognize what is perhaps the biggest driver of energy demand: the human desire to sustain and improve the well-being of ourselves, our families and our communities. Through 2040, population and economic growth will drive demand higher, but the world will use energy more efficiently and shift toward lower-carbon fuels.

25%

The world's population will rise by more than 25 percent from 2010 to 2040, reaching nearly 9 billion people. Population and economic growth are key factors behind increasing demand for energy.

Imagine working for the world's largest publicly traded oil and gas company, on tasks that affect nearly everyone in the world today and for future generations to come. ExxonMobil in the UK is better known for its Esso and Mobil brands due to the success of its service stations and high performance lubricants.

ExxonMobil offers challenging long-term careers to high performing graduates, as well as summer and year placements with real responsibility!

There's no such thing as an average day at ExxonMobil and there are many different career paths available from a technical career to a leadership position to a commercial role. For graduates who are looking for a long-term career that will be challenging, rewarding and certainly varied, then a career with ExxonMobil might just be for them.

What are ExxonMobil looking for? For the technical schemes, applications are welcomed from Chemical, Electrical and Mechanical Engineers with a 2:1 minimum. For the commercial schemes, applications from a number of disciplines including Science/Engineering/IT/Business degrees with a 2:1 minimum are accepted.

In addition to the competitive base salary and relocation allowance, employees are also offered a matched 2-for-1 share scheme, final salary pension plan, private health care scheme, 33 days holiday per annum (including public holidays), interest-free loan, tailored graduate training and continuous development, support towards studying for professional qualifications such as CIMA and IChemE, free sports facilities and subsidised dining facilities at most locations, voluntary community activities, international opportunities and regular job rotations (typically every one to three years) with opportunities to develop and hone skills.

GRADUATE VACANCIES IN 2018

ENGINEERING

NUMBER OF VACANCIES
20-30 graduate jobs

LOCATIONS OF VACANCIES

STARTING SALARY FOR 2018
£38,500+

UNIVERSITY VISITS IN 2017-18
BATH, BIRMINGHAM, CAMBRIDGE, EDINBURGH, IMPERIAL COLLEGE LONDON, LOUGHBOROUGH, MANCHESTER, NEWCASTLE, NOTTINGHAM, SHEFFIELD, SOUTHAMPTON, STRATHCLYDE, SURREY, UNIVERSITY COLLEGE LONDON
Please check with your university careers service for full details of local events.

MINIMUM ENTRY REQUIREMENTS
2.1 Degree

APPLICATION DEADLINE
Year-round recruitment
Early application advised.

FURTHER INFORMATION
www.Top100GraduateEmployers.com
Register now for the latest news, campus events, work experience and graduate vacancies at ExxonMobil.

EY
Building a better
working world

EY is a leading professional services firm helping organisations across the world to navigate complex change. Their community of more than 230,000 people in over 150 countries provides forward-thinking advice to help the firm's clients make better decisions.

What motivates EY is building a better working world – for its people, for its clients and for its communities. Almost everything is being reimagined – technology, innovation and disruption is the norm. Amidst this change, EY is driving innovation, advising its clients on how to change, grow and succeed.

EY combines two essential sets of expertise. The broad, deep business and sector knowledge they're renowned for – assurance, consulting, tax and transactions. This is combined with extensive technology know-how that the firm has built up rapidly in recent years, including investing heavily in world-class technology ecosystem.

This combination of the art of business with the science of technology is what sets EY apart. That, and its people. EY seeks graduates who can see the change the world needs and is excited to be a part of it.

EY offers an incredibly varied range of paths combining study with work, for people of all backgrounds, skills and experiences. From tech-led strategies to women-focused initiatives, EY builds not just partnerships, but successful and fulfilling careers.

The firm believes the key is finding a career path that plays to its people's natural strengths. Identifying these strengths and where they fit in the business world is at the heart of how EY recruits and develops people.

More details of the on-campus sessions EY hosts, plus a wealth of career advice, employability and up-skilling content, are on their website.

GRADUATE VACANCIES IN 2018

ACCOUNTANCY

CONSULTING

FINANCE

IT

NUMBER OF VACANCIES
900 graduate jobs

LOCATIONS OF VACANCIES

STARTING SALARY FOR 2018
£Competitive

UNIVERSITY VISITS IN 2017-18
ABERDEEN, ASTON, BATH, BIRMINGHAM, BRISTOL, CAMBRIDGE, CARDIFF, CITY, DURHAM, EAST ANGLIA, EDINBURGH, EXETER, GLASGOW, HERIOT-WATT, HULL, IMPERIAL COLLEGE LONDON, KING'S COLLEGE LONDON, KENT, LANCASTER, LEEDS, LEICESTER, LIVERPOOL, LONDON SCHOOL OF ECONOMICS, LOUGHBOROUGH, MANCHESTER, NEWCASTLE, NORTHUMBRIA, NOTTINGHAM, NOTTINGHAM TRENT, OXFORD, OXFORD BROOKES, QUEEN MARY LONDON, READING, ROYAL HOLLOWAY, SHEFFIELD, SOUTHAMPTON, ST ANDREWS, STIRLING, STRATHCLYDE, SURREY, SUSSEX, ULSTER, UNIVERSITY COLLEGE LONDON, WARWICK, YORK
Please check with your university careers service for full details of local events.

APPLICATION DEADLINE
Year-round recruitment

FURTHER INFORMATION
www.Top100GraduateEmployers.com
Register now for the latest news, campus events, work experience and graduate vacancies at EY.

Love robotics
but hate being
a robot?

If you're smart and curious, and you want
to shape your career your way, join EY.

Start today. Change tomorrow.
ukcareers.ey.com/graduates

The better the question. The better the answer. The better the world works.

Freshfields

www.freshfields.com/ukgraduates

facebook.com/FreshfieldsGraduates [f]   ukgraduates@freshfields.com [✉]

Freshfields Bruckhaus Deringer advises some of the world's biggest companies on how to grow, strengthen and defend their businesses. For aspiring lawyers keen to pursue a career in commercial law, Freshfields can offer some of the best and most interesting work there is.

Freshfields advise on every type of regulatory issue, from financial services regulation to tax, combating bribery and corruption to buying and selling property; and risk management and disputes work to help defend their clients' businesses and reputations – this involves not only litigation to arbitration but also handling major global investigations by regulatory authorities.

Freshfields divides its business into seven practice groups, which divide further into specialist teams. Trainees must experience at least one seat in corporate, dispute resolution and finance; other seats are available in antitrust, competition and trade; employment, pensions and benefits; real estate; and tax.

Prior to starting a training contract, successful applicants will be supported through their LPC or GDL course. The LPC is available to law students and the GDL is for non-law students. When trainees first arrive there's a two-week induction which includes practical skills workshops and advice to help new trainees hit the ground running. After that, Freshfields offer legal training on a departmental basis and business skills training in how to work productively, delegate and handle pressure.

Throughout a training contract, trainees are offered plenty of guidance. Much of this is on the job working with partners and associates – operating on an open-door policy, so there's always a supportive team around and the opportunity to learn from their fantastic network of lawyers.

GRADUATE VACANCIES IN 2018
LAW

NUMBER OF VACANCIES
Up to 80 graduate jobs
For training contracts starting in 2020.

LOCATIONS OF VACANCIES

STARTING SALARY FOR 2018
£43,000

UNIVERSITY VISITS IN 2017-18
BIRMINGHAM, BRISTOL, CAMBRIDGE, CARDIFF, DURHAM, EDINBURGH, EXETER, GLASGOW, KING'S COLLEGE LONDON, LEEDS, LEICESTER, LONDON SCHOOL OF ECONOMICS, MANCHESTER, NOTTINGHAM, OXFORD, QUEEN MARY LONDON, READING, SHEFFIELD, SOUTHAMPTON, ST ANDREWS, UNIVERSITY COLLEGE LONDON, WARWICK, YORK
Please check with your university careers service for full details of local events.

MINIMUM ENTRY REQUIREMENTS
2.1 Degree

APPLICATION DEADLINE
Varies by function

FURTHER INFORMATION
www.Top100GraduateEmployers.com
Register now for the latest news, campus events, work experience and graduate vacancies at Freshfields.

WE'LL OFFER YOU SUPPORT FROM THE MOMENT YOU ACCEPT A TRAINING CONTRACT TO THE MOMENT YOU QUALIFY – AND BEYOND.

We're one of the world's oldest and most successful law firms, serving businesses from Europe to Asia to the Americas. If you aspire to do high-calibre work for high-quality clients, look no further.

Working for Freshfields isn't always easy and the hours are sometimes long – but you'll be surrounded by dedicated, supportive and ambitious people, who'll lead by example and help you learn.

To find out more, visit
freshfields.com/ukgraduates

FRONTLINE

CHANGING LIVES

There are lots of graduate programmes out there. Most of them involve nice, comfortable office jobs. Frontline is different. The programme represents the only career where graduates can work with all agents across the breadth of a child's life. Participants work with families, schools, courts and the police to change lives.

Changing lives isn't easy. Being a social worker takes resolve, dedication and qualities graduates didn't even know they had. Most people would probably run in the opposite direction. But for those few who dare to change; who want one of Britain's most challenging but rewarding jobs, then Frontline is for them.

Frontline's two-year leadership development programme is a unique opportunity for exceptional individuals to join one of Britain's toughest and most rewarding professions – child protection social work. Social work is the only career which provides the chance to work with such a wide variety of organisations, impacting on every aspect of a child and their family's life.

The programme begins with a five-week summer residential where a team of world-leading academics and individuals with care experience deliver master classes in social work practice. In September, participants join a local authority and start their first year, learning 'on-the-job' while receiving ongoing academic tuition. Upon qualification, the second year consists of 12 months guaranteed employment as a children's social worker and the opportunity to study towards a fully funded Masters qualification.

Participants will work in child protection teams in Greater London, the Midlands, the North West, the North East and the South East. Frontline is committed to developing leadership skills amongst participants so they can drive positive change both in social work and in broader society. Frontline welcomes applications from students from a range of degree disciplines.

GRADUATE VACANCIES IN 2018

GENERAL MANAGEMENT

HUMAN RESOURCES

LAW

NUMBER OF VACANCIES
352 graduate jobs

LOCATIONS OF VACANCIES

STARTING SALARY FOR 2018
£Competitive

UNIVERSITY VISITS IN 2017-18
ASTON, BATH, BIRMINGHAM, BRADFORD, BRISTOL, CAMBRIDGE, CARDIFF, CITY, DURHAM, EDINBURGH, ESSEX, EXETER, KING'S COLLEGE LONDON, KENT, LANCASTER, LEEDS, LEICESTER, LIVERPOOL, LONDON SCHOOL OF ECONOMICS, LOUGHBOROUGH, MANCHESTER, NEWCASTLE, NORTHUMBRIA, NOTTINGHAM, OXFORD, QUEEN MARY LONDON, SHEFFIELD, SOUTHAMPTON, ST ANDREWS, SUSSEX, UNIVERSITY COLLEGE LONDON, WARWICK, YORK
Please check with your university careers service for full details of local events.

MINIMUM ENTRY REQUIREMENTS
2.1 Degree

APPLICATION DEADLINE
20th November 2017

FURTHER INFORMATION
www.Top100GraduateEmployers.com
Register now for the latest news, campus events, work experience and graduate vacancies at **Frontline***.*

"My most rewarding experience so far was when after months of working with a family and tackling different issues, a mother told me how much she felt supported by having me in her life. That was a special moment."

- Margaret, 2015 participant

FRONTLINE

Frontline recruits outstanding individuals to be leaders in social work and broader society. On our intensive and innovative two year leadership development programme you will gain a master's degree and work to transform the lives of vulnerable children, young people and their families.

www.thefrontline.org.uk

GRADUATE VACANCIES IN 2018

CONSULTING
ENGINEERING
FINANCE
GENERAL MANAGEMENT
IT
RESEARCH & DEVELOPMENT

NUMBER OF VACANCIES
200+ graduate jobs

LOCATIONS OF VACANCIES

GCHQ, Britain's signals intelligence agency, plays a major role in protecting the country's people, businesses and infrastructure. Think terrorism, espionage, organised crime and cyber attacks. Using technical expertise and intelligence to counter these threats, graduates can expect a truly fascinating career.

As Britain faces increasingly sophisticated threats, GCHQ constantly develops unique and creative solutions to stay one step ahead of adversaries. GCHQ intelligence helps keep British forces safe, prevents terrorism, crime and protects Britain against cyber attacks.

GCHQ has a diverse workforce and is looking for graduates with different skills, backgrounds and perspectives to share its commitment to keeping Britain safe, secure and successful. Graduates joining GCHQ can expect challenging projects, early responsibility, outstanding professional development and a rewarding career experience.

GCHQ is proud of its mission and its people. Its working culture encourages open minds and attitudes and is supported by a welfare and benefits structure that enables its workforce to be at its best. From extensive training and development that enables employees to expand their skills, to the flexibility to explore different roles, tools and technologies, a career at GCHQ offers graduates a unique opportunity and supports them to achieve their full potential.

Graduate careers are varied, including technology, analysis, and languages, as well as corporate roles including project management, finance and leadership. Students can take advantage of a variety of summer placements, including Languages and Maths, as well as a Cyber Summer School. Bursaries are also offered to those who plan to, or already study a STEM subject at university.

Due to the sensitive nature of the work applicants must be British citizens.

STARTING SALARY FOR 2018
£25,000+
Additional bonuses and allowances may be payable depending on skills and experience.

MINIMUM ENTRY REQUIREMENTS
2.2 Degree

APPLICATION DEADLINE
Year-round recruitment

FURTHER INFORMATION
www.Top100GraduateEmployers.com
Register now for the latest news, campus events, work experience and graduate vacancies at GCHQ.

WE'RE IN A CLASS OF OUR OWN.

Find out why.

Various
Opportunities

GCHQ

Make a complex world yours

Goldman Sachs is a leading global investment banking, securities and investment management firm that provides a wide range of financial services to a substantial and diversified client base, including corporations, financial institutions, governments and individuals.

At Goldman Sachs, graduates have many opportunities to make an impact. The unique perspectives that its people bring to the firm and their shared passion for working on projects of great global, economic and social significance, help drive progress and create results.

Goldman Sachs is structured in a series of divisions: Consumer and Commercial Banking, Executive Office, Finance, Global Compliance, Global Investment Research, Human Capital Management, Internal Audit, Investment Banking, Investment Management, Legal, Merchant Banking, Operations, Realty Management, Risk, Securities, Services and Technology.

From the first day, graduates will be immersed in a collaborative environment with people of all levels who share the firm's values. Nearly everyone – from junior analysts to the most senior leaders – is actively involved in recruiting talented people from a variety of backgrounds, because the firm recognises that a diverse workforce enables them to serve its clients most effectively and in the most innovative ways.

The diversity of talents and educational backgrounds in its people is crucial to performance and business success. To that end, Goldman Sachs is committed to an environment that values diversity, promotes inclusion and encourages teamwork.

Whatever the background or area of academic study, Goldman Sachs values the intellect, personality and integrity of an individual. While an interest in and appreciation for finance is important, one's personal qualities are key.

GRADUATE VACANCIES IN 2018
INVESTMENT BANKING

NUMBER OF VACANCIES
Around 300 graduate jobs

LOCATIONS OF VACANCIES

Vacancies also available in Europe.

STARTING SALARY FOR 2018
£Competitive
Plus an attractive benefits package.

UNIVERSITY VISITS IN 2017-18
BATH, BRISTOL, CAMBRIDGE, DURHAM, EDINBURGH, GLASGOW, IMPERIAL COLLEGE LONDON, KING'S COLLEGE LONDON, LONDON SCHOOL OF ECONOMICS, LOUGHBOROUGH, MANCHESTER, NOTTINGHAM, OXFORD, READING, TRINITY COLLEGE DUBLIN, UNIVERSITY COLLEGE DUBLIN, UNIVERSITY COLLEGE LONDON, WARWICK
Please check with your university careers service for full details of local events.

APPLICATION DEADLINE
29th October 2017

FURTHER INFORMATION
www.Top100GraduateEmployers.com
Register now for the latest news, campus events, work experience and graduate vacancies at Goldman Sachs.

Goldman Sachs

HOW WILL YOU
MAKE AN IMPACT

CONTRIBUTE, COLLABORATE AND SUCCEED WITH A CAREER AT GOLDMAN SACHS

If you're the kind of person who can't wait to make a difference, consider a career at Goldman Sachs. We believe that good ideas and innovations can come from anyone, at any level. We offer meaningful opportunities, best-in-class training and a wide variety of career paths for talented people from all academic backgrounds. Plus, with access to important clients and projects, you'll have the chance to make an impact with global significance.

APPLICATION DEADLINES

NEW ANALYST: Sunday 29 October 2017
SUMMER ANALYST: Sunday 3 December 2017
SPRING PROGRAMME: Wednesday 3 January 2018
WORK PLACEMENT PROGRAMME: Wednesday 3 January 2018
For Warsaw-specific deadlines please visit the website

Submit your application at
goldmansachs.com/careers

goldmansachs.com/careers
 @GSCareers

Google

Founders Larry Page and Sergey Brin met at Stanford University in 1995. By 1996, they had built a search engine that used links to determine the importance of individual web pages. Today, Google is a tech company that helps businesses of all kinds succeed on and off the web.

It's really the people that make Google the kind of company it is. Google hires people who are smart and determined, and favour ability over experience. Google's mission is to increase access to information, and our approach to diversity is a natural extension of that mission: to increase access to opportunity by breaking down barriers and empowering people through technology. The diversity of perspectives, ideas, and cultures, both within Google and in the tech industry overall, leads to the creation of better products and services.

University graduates joining Google will enter either the Google Marketing Solutions (GMS) Sales or Global Customer Experience teams. As small business experts, Googlers in GMS help to get local entrepreneurs on the map, and deliver a simple, intuitive experience that enables customers to grow their businesses. By spotting and analysing customer needs and trends, Google's innovative teams of strategists, account developers and customer experience specialists work together on scalable solutions for each business, no matter its age or size.

Google hires graduates from all disciplines, from humanities and business related courses to engineering and computer science. The ideal candidate is someone who can demonstrate a passion for the online industry and someone who has made the most of their time at university through involvement in clubs, societies or relevant internships. Google hires graduates who have a variety of strengths and passions, not just isolated skill sets. For technical roles within engineering teams, specific skills will be required.

GRADUATE VACANCIES IN 2018
CONSULTING
ENGINEERING
HUMAN RESOURCES
IT
MARKETING
MEDIA
SALES

NUMBER OF VACANCIES
No fixed quota

LOCATIONS OF VACANCIES

Vacancies also available in Europe and the USA.

STARTING SALARY FOR 2018
£Competitive
Plus world-renowned perks and benefits.

UNIVERSITY VISITS IN 2017-18
Please check with your university careers service for full details of local events.

MINIMUM ENTRY REQUIREMENTS
2.1 Degree

APPLICATION DEADLINE
Year-round recruitment

FURTHER INFORMATION
www.Top100GraduateEmployers.com
Register now for the latest news, campus events, work experience and graduate vacancies at Google.

BRING QUESTIONS

BUILD ANSWERS

Google

www.google.com/careers/students

SHAPE
MORE THAN JUST YOUR
CAREER

What if there was a new way of doing business? Where profit and purpose combine to drive sustainable growth for businesses and wider society. Grant Thornton are an organisation thinking differently about everything they do. Graduates joining them will get to do the same.

There's never been a more exciting time to be a part of a firm that are passionate about their purpose – shaping a vibrant economy in the UK and beyond. Grant Thornton has a unique culture built around a shared enterprise model. Their people are empowered to share ideas, share responsibility and share in the subsequent rewards.

They're a global organisation offering business and financial advice to dynamic organisations in countries all over the world. Working with organisations of all sizes, from multinationals to start-ups, building trust and integrity in markets, unlocking sustainable growth and creating environments where businesses and people thrive.

Graduates join on a three-year programme to become professionally qualified advisers, specialising in either advisory, audit or tax. Through structured training, varied on-the-ground client experience and a supportive working environment, trainees get the chance to develop and grow as trusted advisers with a deep understanding of business, as well as achieving a respected professional qualification and a competitive salary.

Trainee business advisers at Grant Thornton are credible, agile and passionate about what they do – working with dynamic clients and building strong relationships quickly. All of their graduates are inspired to make a difference and encouraged to bring unique ideas – knowing what they do matters to clients and their business and in shaping a vibrant economy.

GRADUATE VACANCIES IN 2018

ACCOUNTANCY
CONSULTING
FINANCE

NUMBER OF VACANCIES
200 graduate jobs

LOCATIONS OF VACANCIES

STARTING SALARY FOR 2018
£Competitive

UNIVERSITY VISITS IN 2017-18
ASTON, BIRMINGHAM, BRISTOL, CARDIFF, CITY, DURHAM, EAST ANGLIA, EXETER, GLASGOW, KENT, LEEDS, LEICESTER, LIVERPOOL, LOUGHBOROUGH, MANCHESTER, NOTTINGHAM, OXFORD BROOKES, READING, WARWICK, YORK
Please check with your university careers service for full details of local events.

APPLICATION DEADLINE
Varies by function

FURTHER INFORMATION
www.Top100GraduateEmployers.com
Register now for the latest news, campus events, work experience and graduate vacancies at **Grant Thornton***.*

SHAPE
MORE THAN JUST YOUR
CAREER

At Grant Thornton, we think differently about everything we do. Join us and do the same. Your ideas will be implemented. Your opinions heard. Your contributions valued. Not just by your colleagues, but by coveted clients. Come and share in our bold and ambitious vision of shaping a vibrant economy for the UK and beyond. We're looking for independent thinkers and future business advisers to inspire changes that can be felt far wider than our business. So bring your passion, ambitions and inspiration, and together let's make it happen.

trainees.grant-thornton.co.uk

 Grant Thornton | An instinct for growth™

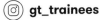 **gt_trainees**

GSK is a science-led global healthcare company of over 100,000 individuals united by their mission and four values of patient focus, integrity, respect for people and transparency. GSK put these values at the heart of everything they do to better help meet their patients and consumers needs.

Based in the UK, with operations in over 115 countries, GSK research and develop a broad range of healthcare products from lifesaving prescription medicines and vaccines to popular consumer products such as Beechams, Sensodyne, Savlon and Panadol. Every year GSK screens millions of compounds and make billions of packs of medicines and consumer healthcare products, with a commitment to widening access to their products, so more people can benefit, no matter where they live in the world or what they can afford to pay.

Dedicated to helping millions of people around the world to do more, feel better and live longer, GSK is revolutionising its business to meet changing global healthcare needs. GSK invested £3.6 billion in R&D in 2016 and has consistently topped the Access to Medicine Index, reinforcing the company's commitment to tackle some of the world's worst diseases by embracing new, open and innovative ways of working.

GSK is deeply committed to developing people through a range of ongoing opportunities that includes tailored 2-3 year rotational graduate Future Leaders programmes, industrial or summer placements. Successful graduates will be stretched to forge new relationships, seek out new experiences and be responsible for driving their own development. GSK will be there every step of the way, helping to build the skills that will allow them to reach their potential.

Most of all, GSK graduates enjoy the sense of purpose that comes from leading change in an industry that touches millions every day.

GRADUATE VACANCIES IN 2018

ACCOUNTANCY
CONSULTING
ENGINEERING
FINANCE
GENERAL MANAGEMENT
HUMAN RESOURCES
IT
LOGISTICS
MARKETING
PURCHASING
RESEARCH & DEVELOPMENT
SALES

NUMBER OF VACANCIES
70+ graduate jobs

LOCATIONS OF VACANCIES

Vacancies also available in Europe, the USA, Asia and elsewhere in the world.

STARTING SALARY FOR 2018
£Competitive
Plus a relocation allowance.

UNIVERSITY VISITS IN 2017-18
BATH, BIRMINGHAM, BRUNEL, CAMBRIDGE, CARDIFF, EDINBURGH, EXETER, IMPERIAL COLLEGE LONDON, KING'S COLLEGE LONDON, LEEDS, LOUGHBOROUGH, MANCHESTER, OXFORD, QUEEN MARY LONDON, SHEFFIELD, SOUTHAMPTON, STRATHCLYDE, WARWICK
Please check with your university careers service for full details of local events.

MINIMUM ENTRY REQUIREMENTS
2.1 Degree

APPLICATION DEADLINE
Varies by function

FURTHER INFORMATION
www.Top100GraduateEmployers.com
Register now for the latest news, campus events, work experience and graduate vacancies at GSK.

gsk
do more
feel better
live longer

Lead change.
Benefit millions of lives.

Join our Future Leaders Programme
and you'll be part of a leading
global business tackling the world's
biggest healthcare challenges. Bring
your curiosity. Share our ambition.
We'll give you the opportunities
to build the future you want.

Find out more at
www.futureleaders.gsk.com

Yazmin
IT Future Leaders Programme.
Ensuring leading IT systems
protect patient safety.

careers.herbertsmithfreehills.com/uk/grads

graduates.UK@hsf.com ✉
twitter.com/HSFgraduatesUK 🐦   facebook.com/HSFgrads f
linkedin.com/company/herbert-smith-freehills in   youtube.com/HSFlegal ▶

World-class disputes practice. Market-leading corporate practice. Top-tier specialist teams. Herbert Smith Freehills has got it all. A global elite law firm, they work with some of the largest international organisations on their most ambitious projects.

With over 3,000 lawyers in 26 offices across Asia, Australia, Europe, the Middle East and the USA, working across borders is a key part of their philosophy. This gives trainees the chance to work in a truly international way.

The work is incredibly varied. Herbert Smith Freehills provides top quality tailored legal advice to major corporations, commercial organisations, financial institutions and governments. They advise more FTSE 100 clients than any other UK or US-headquartered firm. Their dispute resolution practice is number one in the UK, Asia and Australia and includes their leading international arbitration practice and award-winning in-house advocacy unit. They can therefore offer a complete litigation service and a realistic alternative to the Bar.

That's not all. Other practice areas include Finance, Competition, Regulation and Trade, Real Estate and Employment, Pensions and Incentives as well as specialist areas like Intellectual Property and Tax.

Herbert Smith Freehills' trainees are a part of everything. The training contract balances contentious and non-contentious work with pro bono opportunities and real responsibility. Trainees rotate around four six-month seats with the opportunity to go on secondment to a client or an international office.

The firm offers global exposure and a supportive network. Trainees will focus on technical excellence and a client-led approach. Those who have the drive, ambition and potential to seize the opportunities on offer and become a brilliant lawyer, shouldn't compromise. Be a part of everything at Herbert Smith Freehills.

GRADUATE VACANCIES IN 2018
LAW

NUMBER OF VACANCIES
60 graduate jobs
For training contracts starting in 2020.

LOCATIONS OF VACANCIES

Vacancies also available in Europe, the USA, Asia and elsewhere in the world.

STARTING SALARY FOR 2018
£44,000

UNIVERSITY VISITS IN 2017-18
BIRMINGHAM, BRISTOL, CAMBRIDGE, CARDIFF, DURHAM, EDINBURGH, EXETER, GLASGOW, SOUTHAMPTON, ST ANDREWS, WARWICK, YORK
Please check with your university careers service for full details of local events.

MINIMUM ENTRY REQUIREMENTS
2.1 Degree

APPLICATION DEADLINE
Year-round recruitment
Early application advised.

FURTHER INFORMATION
www.Top100GraduateEmployers.com
*Register now for the latest news, campus events, work experience and graduate vacancies at **Herbert Smith Freehills**.*

**HERBERT
SMITH
FREEHILLS**

LEGAL CAREERS
BEYOND BORDERS

BE A PART OF EVERYTHING

EXPLORE A PROGRESSIVE FIRM
WITH GLOBAL CONNECTIONS

Deep insight. International foundations. A non-hierarchical network.
At Herbert Smith Freehills, we work with some of the world's biggest
organisations on ambitious, complex and high-profile projects. From
cross-border deals to headline disputes, we're providing award-winning
advice on matters that will shape the future of the law. Join us and
together we can change the way the legal world works.

SEARCH **HSF GRADUATES**

26
OFFICES
GLOBALLY

220
INTERNATIONAL
SECONDMENTS

£44k
IN FIRST
YEAR

Hogan Lovells

A practical, straight-talking approach to law. Open, honest and deep relationships with clients. Training that keeps on evolving. A global community where everyone is on the same wavelength – but always encouraged to be themselves. All of this gives Hogan Lovells a different dynamic to other global law firms.

It's why many prestigious, forward-thinking clients choose to work with them. The firm has a reputation not just for the consistently high quality of its 2,500 lawyers, but also for its sense of community. The network of over 45 global offices collaborates closely. Together, their teams of corporate, finance, dispute resolution, government regulatory and intellectual property lawyers tackle some of the most intricate legal and commercial issues that businesses face.

Here, trainee solicitors don't just master law. They develop industry expertise and explore the principles of business, entrepreneurship and social enterprise.

Each year, the firm takes on up to 60 trainee solicitors – both law and non-law graduates. The two-year training contract is split into four six-month 'seats'. During this time, trainee solicitors move around four different practice areas, including corporate, finance, and dispute resolution. Graduates will gain exposure to and develop a rounded understanding of international law, and they will have an opportunity to apply for an international or client secondment.

Hogan Lovells also runs highly-regarded spring, summer and winter vacation schemes. Up to 65 places are available in total. Each lasts up to three weeks, and gives participants the chance to work alongside partners, associates and trainees in major practice areas. Students are exposed to two or three practice areas and learn to draft documents, carry out legal research, attend meetings and in some cases attend court. This hands-on learning is complemented by tailored workshops, case studies and social events.

GRADUATE VACANCIES IN 2018
LAW

NUMBER OF VACANCIES
60 graduate jobs
For training contracts starting in 2020.

LOCATIONS OF VACANCIES

STARTING SALARY FOR 2018
£44,000

UNIVERSITY VISITS IN 2017-18
BELFAST, BIRMINGHAM, BRISTOL, CAMBRIDGE, CARDIFF, DURHAM, EAST ANGLIA, EXETER, HULL, KING'S COLLEGE LONDON, LANCASTER, LEEDS, LEICESTER, LONDON SCHOOL OF ECONOMICS, MANCHESTER, NEWCASTLE, NOTTINGHAM, OXFORD, QUEEN MARY LONDON, SHEFFIELD, SOUTHAMPTON, ST ANDREWS, TRINITY COLLEGE DUBLIN, UNIVERSITY COLLEGE DUBLIN, UNIVERSITY COLLEGE LONDON, WARWICK, YORK
Please check with your university careers service for full details of local events.

MINIMUM ENTRY REQUIREMENTS
2.1 Degree

APPLICATION DEADLINE
Law: 31st July 2018
Non-law: 31st January 2018

FURTHER INFORMATION
www.Top100GraduateEmployers.com
Register now for the latest news, campus events, work experience and graduate vacancies at Hogan Lovells.

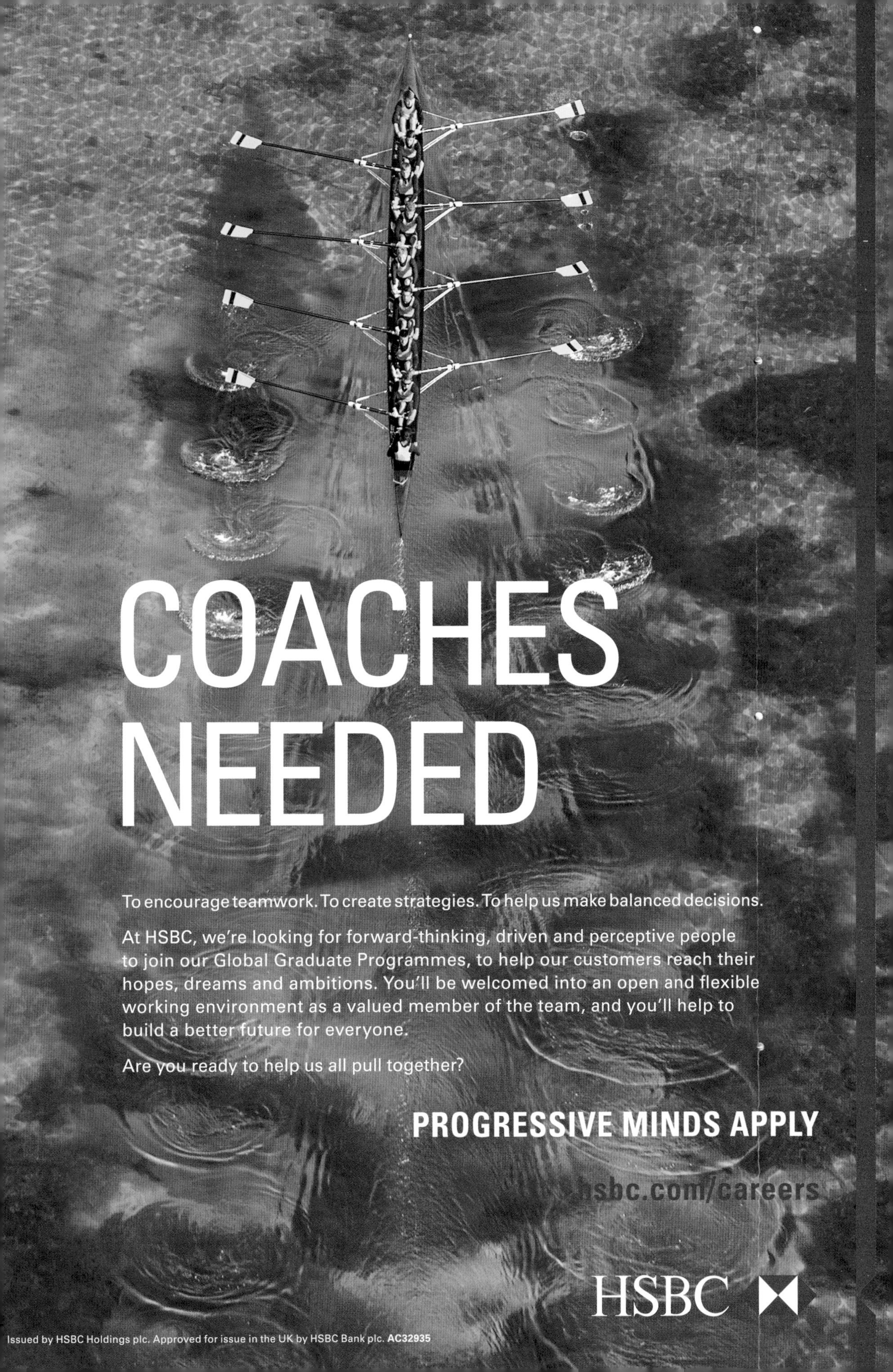
COACHES NEEDED
To encourage teamwork. To create strategies. To help us make balanced decisions.
At HSBC, we're looking for forward-thinking, driven and perceptive people to join our Global Graduate Programmes, to help our customers reach their hopes, dreams and ambitions. You'll be welcomed into an open and flexible working environment as a valued member of the team, and you'll help to build a better future for everyone.
Are you ready to help us all pull together?
PROGRESSIVE MINDS APPLY
hsbc.com/careers
HSBC
Issued by HSBC Holdings plc. Approved for issue in the UK by HSBC Bank plc. AC32935

GRADUATE VACANCIES IN 2018
CONSULTING
IT
SALES

NUMBER OF VACANCIES
300+ graduate jobs

LOCATIONS OF VACANCIES

IBM are looking for passionate graduates interested in developing their skills and building their career with a global leader. At IBM graduates get the support needed to make a real impact and most importantly they will have the opportunity to do work that matters.

IBM work with some of the greatest and best known names on the planet, providing IT services and consultancy across all industries including retail, sport, business, finance, health, media and entertainment.

IBM look for the best and brightest graduates, from all universities, degree backgrounds and abilities. They want creative and passionate people who will share their dedication to tackling the world's toughest problems. Whether graduates want to pursue a career in consulting, technology, business, design or sales they'll have the chance to collaborate with extraordinary people in a creative environment to make the world work better.

IBM are dedicated to giving graduates every opportunity to enhance their career development. They'll work in an environment that cultivates creativity and individual differences, rewarding their best work.

IBM's award-winning, bespoke training is designed to give graduates the personal, business and technical skills to take their career wherever they want to go. Graduates will continuously learn and develop new skills and have the opportunity to contribute to the enhancement of their field.

IBM will encourage graduates to extend their expertise through customised professional development and leadership training, allocating every graduate a professional development manager and a mentor to ensure graduates get the most out of the programme.

Be part of a global transformation and join IBM.

STARTING SALARY FOR 2018
£30,000
Plus medical, pension and stock purchase plans, stock equity awards, a laptop and 25 days holiday.

UNIVERSITY VISITS IN 2017-18
BATH, BIRMINGHAM, CARDIFF, DURHAM, EDINBURGH, EXETER, IMPERIAL COLLEGE LONDON, LANCASTER, LEEDS, LOUGHBOROUGH, MANCHESTER, NOTTINGHAM, OXFORD, SOUTHAMPTON, UNIVERSITY COLLEGE LONDON
Please check with your university careers service for full details of local events.

MINIMUM ENTRY REQUIREMENTS
2.1 Degree

APPLICATION DEADLINE
Year-round recruitment
Early application advised.

FURTHER INFORMATION
www.Top100GraduateEmployers.com
Register now for the latest news, campus events, work experience and graduate vacancies at IBM.

I work where
I am encouraged
to push boundaries.

ibm.com/jobs/uk

IM, irwinmitchell
solicitors

www.irwinmitchell.com/graduates

www.irwinmitchell.com/graduates

twitter.com/IMGraduates

graduaterecruitment@irwinmitchell.com

The Irwin Mitchell Group is one of a few law firms to provide a diverse range of legal services to business and private clients. It has a strong customer service culture and a high level of client retention. Following the merger with Thomas Eggar in December 2015, national presence has increased to 15 locations.

The firm's training contracts are streamed so that a trainee solicitor would either undertake a training contract based within the Personal Legal Services or Business Legal Services division. As a national firm, there is opportunity to undertake a training contract in one or more locations in the UK. Trainees will have three training seats and a qualification seat, giving them the chance to gain practical experience in diverse areas of law, whilst maximising retention opportunities. Whatever division is chosen, trainees will enjoy a fantastic training contract at a truly unique and innovative firm.

Irwin Mitchell seek to provide opportunities to those who have the ability to work under pressure in a fast paced environment. The trainees will be creatively minded, use their initiative and have strong organisational and problem solving skills.

From the moment a trainee joins Irwin Mitchell they will receive a dedicated training and development programme. The firm invests in the future of employees, as this could build their journey to the very top of the firm.

Each summer the firm runs a formal work placement programme which is a great way to get a real insight into what life is like as a trainee at Irwin Mitchell, along with the culture. An increasing number of training contracts are offered to those who have undertaken a Legal Work Placement, so all those interested in joining should apply via this route.

GRADUATE VACANCIES IN 2018
LAW

NUMBER OF VACANCIES
45 graduate jobs
For training contracts starting in 2020.

LOCATIONS OF VACANCIES

STARTING SALARY FOR 2018
£25,000+
Plus GDL/LPC fees and a maintenance grant.

UNIVERSITY VISITS IN 2017-18
BIRMINGHAM, BRISTOL, CARDIFF, EXETER, LEEDS, LIVERPOOL, MANCHESTER, NEWCASTLE, NOTTINGHAM, SHEFFIELD, SOUTHAMPTON, WARWICK, YORK
Please check with your university careers service for full details of local events.

MINIMUM ENTRY REQUIREMENTS
2.1 Degree
320 UCAS points

APPLICATION DEADLINE
30th June 2018

FURTHER INFORMATION
www.Top100GraduateEmployers.com
Register now for the latest news, campus events, work experience and graduate vacancies at **Irwin Mitchell**.

140 TOP 100 GRADUATE EMPLOYERS

Jaguar Land Rover is one of the automotive world's most compelling success stories. It is a British technology company with a global reach, and as the UK's largest car manufacturer, it is now producing and selling more cars than at any time in its history.

But there are still ambitious plans for more profitable, sustainable growth around the world. So finding the next generation of innovators, bright and passionate people is crucial. It is relying on the pioneering spirit of its workforce to help invent the future. So to keep that momentum going, any new recruits need a creative and commercially focused approach to their work. Bring that and Jaguar Land Rover has all the opportunities and rewards that graduates want and need.

But opportunities do not stop there. The graduate scheme has been designed to be as inspiring as the vehicles successful applicants will help to design, engineer and sell. As the UK's largest investor in research and innovation, education is a critical part of Jaguar Land Rover's business strategy and ambition. It aims to hire the best talent and, then, through a lifelong education and training programmes, help those people fulfil their potential. These opportunities lie right across the business from engineering, manufacturing and software design, to commercial and business areas.

As would be expected from two of the world's most revered brands, a range of rewards and benefits await those who have the initiative, vision and drive to contribute to the organisation's global success – including a competitive salary, joining bonus, pension scheme and discount car purchase scheme. All this and more makes Jaguar Land Rover an enviable place for graduates to start their journey.

GRADUATE VACANCIES IN 2018

ACCOUNTANCY
ENGINEERING
FINANCE
HUMAN RESOURCES
IT
LOGISTICS
MARKETING
PROPERTY
PURCHASING
RESEARCH & DEVELOPMENT

NUMBER OF VACANCIES
250-300 graduate jobs

LOCATIONS OF VACANCIES

STARTING SALARY FOR 2018
£29,000
Plus a £2,000 joining bonus.

UNIVERSITY VISITS IN 2017-18
ASTON, BATH, BELFAST, BIRMINGHAM, BRISTOL, BRUNEL, CAMBRIDGE, CARDIFF, DURHAM, EDINBURGH, EXETER, GLASGOW, IMPERIAL COLLEGE LONDON, LANCASTER, LEEDS, LEICESTER, LIVERPOOL, LOUGHBOROUGH, MANCHESTER, NOTTINGHAM, OXFORD, SHEFFIELD, SOUTHAMPTON, STRATHCLYDE, TRINITY COLLEGE DUBLIN, UNIVERSITY COLLEGE DUBLIN, WARWICK, YORK
Please check with your university careers service for full details of local events.

MINIMUM ENTRY REQUIREMENTS
2.2 Degree
Relevant degree required for some roles.

APPLICATION DEADLINE
31st December 2017

FURTHER INFORMATION
www.Top100GraduateEmployers.com
Register now for the latest news, campus events, work experience and graduate vacancies at Jaguar Land Rover.

BOLD. BOLDER. BOLDEST.

GRADUATE & UNDERGRADUATE OPPORTUNITIES
ENGINEERING & COMMERCIAL BUSINESS AREAS

We're on a journey. A journey to redefine the benchmark for excellence. With ambitions to set pulses racing in more countries and more markets than ever before, there's never been a more exciting time to join. The scale of our ambition is reflected by the ever-expanding breadth of our graduate programmes and undergraduate placements. From our Manufacturing and Engineering disciplines to our Commercial and Business functions, this is a place where you'll continually push the boundaries of your own potential. Where you'll develop specialist and commercial skills working alongside an industry-revered team. Where your achievements, and ours, will only go from strength to strength to strength.

Discover careers that move at **jaguarlandrovercareers.com**

J.P.Morgan

Banking is a vital part of the world's economy and everyday life. Over the last 200 years J.P. Morgan has evolved as a business to meet the ever-changing needs of some of the world's largest companies as well as many of the smaller businesses that are a cornerstone of local communities. They work tirelessly to do the right thing for their clients, shareholders and the firm every day.

J.P. Morgan's strength lies not only in the quality of its products, but also within the invaluable power of its employees. Harnessing the diversity of its people, J.P. Morgan values those with different talents, ranging from investment banking to technology, operations and human resources.

Career opportunities are available across the firm, so it pays to learn as much as possible about the industry, business areas and the roles available. Be sure to take advantage of pre-internship programmes, such as Insight Days and Spring Week, which give students a chance to get noticed early – many interns are hired directly from the Spring Week programme.

J.P. Morgan offers internship and graduate opportunities in the following areas: Asset Management, Global Finance & Business Management, Global Treasury Management, Human Resources, Investment Banking, Investor Services Sales, Markets, Operations, Quantitative Research, Risk Management, Technology and Wealth Management.

J.P. Morgan is looking for collaborative future leaders who have passion, creativity and exceptional interpersonal skills. Impeccable academic credentials are important, but so are achievements outside the classroom.

Working with a team committed to doing their best, earning the trust of their clients and encouraging employees to fulfil their potential. That's what it means to be part of J.P. Morgan.

GRADUATE VACANCIES IN 2018

FINANCE
HUMAN RESOURCES
INVESTMENT BANKING
IT

NUMBER OF VACANCIES
400+ graduate jobs

LOCATIONS OF VACANCIES

STARTING SALARY FOR 2018
£Competitive

UNIVERSITY VISITS IN 2017-18
BATH, CAMBRIDGE, EDINBURGH, EXETER, GLASGOW, IMPERIAL COLLEGE LONDON, LONDON SCHOOL OF ECONOMICS, OXFORD, SOUTHAMPTON, ST ANDREWS, STRATHCLYDE, UNIVERSITY COLLEGE LONDON, WARWICK
Please check with your university careers service for full details of local events.

MINIMUM ENTRY REQUIREMENTS
2.1 Degree

APPLICATION DEADLINE
26th November 2017

FURTHER INFORMATION
www.Top100GraduateEmployers.com
Register now for the latest news, campus events, work experience and graduate vacancies at J.P. Morgan.

www.kpmgcareers.co.uk

facebook.com/kpmgrecruitment **f**   ukfmgraduate@kpmg.co.uk ✉

kpmgcareers.co.uk/linkedin **in**   twitter.com/kpmgrecruitment **y**

youtube.com/kpmgrecruitmentuk ▶   instagram.com/kpmgtraineesuk ◉

KPMG is one of the UK's largest providers of Audit, Tax and Consulting services. Working with start-ups to major multinationals, private and public sector, applying insight and expertise to help solve its clients' biggest issues. Part of a global network, it employs over 13,000 people across the UK.

KPMG's Audit, Tax, Consultancy, Deal Advisory, Technology and Business Services programmes offer graduates the chance to work with some of the brightest minds and reach their full potential. KPMG offers a breadth of experience across a range of industries such as Retail, Leisure, Charities, Banking, Government and the Public Sector.

Delivering innovative approaches calls for diverse perspectives; KPMG welcomes a range of personalities, skill sets and degree disciplines. Thanks to The Academy – a unique learning community created to help trainees develop through workshops and networking events – the support trainees receive is as individual as they are. What's more, the full-time Professional Qualification Training and Accreditation team is also on hand to help trainees to pass professional exams.

To succeed in an ever-changing, and increasingly digital business world, today's graduates need resilience, curiosity and the motivation for continuous improvement. At KPMG, trainees are rewarded for their contributions with development opportunities and a host of great benefits, including access to preferential banking and cash towards student loan payments.

The rewards of a career with KPMG begin early with Launch Pad, an innovative, streamlined approach to the recruitment process, it allows graduate candidates to enjoy a meaningful experience while securing a job offer earlier than ever. In short, KPMG is an award-winning employer, where graduates can learn, grow and thrive.

GRADUATE VACANCIES IN 2018

ACCOUNTANCY
CONSULTING
FINANCE
GENERAL MANAGEMENT
HUMAN RESOURCES
IT
MARKETING

NUMBER OF VACANCIES
Around 1,000 graduate jobs

LOCATIONS OF VACANCIES

STARTING SALARY FOR 2018
£Competitive
Plus great benefits, including access to preferential banking and cash towards student loan payments.

UNIVERSITY VISITS IN 2017-18
ABERDEEN, ASTON, BIRMINGHAM, BRISTOL, CAMBRIDGE, CARDIFF, CITY, DUNDEE, EXETER, GLASGOW, HERIOT-WATT, KING'S COLLEGE LONDON, LEEDS, LEICESTER, LIVERPOOL, MANCHESTER, NEWCASTLE, NOTTINGHAM TRENT, OXFORD, QUEEN MARY LONDON, READING, ROYAL HOLLOWAY, SHEFFIELD, ST ANDREWS, STRATHCLYDE, UNIVERSITY COLLEGE LONDON, WARWICK
Please check with your university careers service for full details of local events.

MINIMUM ENTRY REQUIREMENTS
2.1 Degree
300 UCAS points
However, it's not just academic performance KPMG is interested in. Please see website for specific programme requirements.

APPLICATION DEADLINE
Year-round recruitment
Early application advised.

FURTHER INFORMATION
www.Top100GraduateEmployers.com
Register now for the latest news, campus events, work experience and graduate vacancies at KPMG.

Curiosity loves company.

At KPMG in the UK you can work side-by-side with some of the brightest minds in business, full of innovative ideas and natural curiosity. With the opportunity to learn every day, you'll be encouraged to be yourself, focused on delivering results for our people, clients and communities.

So whether your journey of discovery leads to Audit, Tax, Consultancy, Deal Advisory, Technology or Business Services, we will value your contribution, and believe we can satisfy your ambition.

kpmgcareers.co.uk/graduates

Anticipate tomorrow. Deliver today.

Think 32 iconic international brands, selling in 130 countries. Think Ralph Lauren. Think Diesel. Think Garnier. Think Urban Decay. And now, think about the change graduates can bring, when they work for the world's number one cosmetics group. It's time to lead the change at L'Oréal.

At the forefront of a booming £10 billion industry in the UK, L'Oréal continues to invent and revolutionise. In 2016, the group registered a stunning 473 patents for newly invented products and formulae. That constant creativity, and determined exploration of every possibility, is what makes L'Oréal a global success symbol.

So, when it comes to their Management Trainee Programme, L'Oréal need more than just graduates. They need inventors, explorers, leaders, and entrepreneurs. Graduates who know that when it comes to success, inspirational talent and hard work go hand in hand. Graduates who know that they should never stop exploring. L'Oréal believes in developing their talent from the ground up, providing their employees with the opportunity to grow within the company and build a career. This is why 100% of their Management Trainee roles are filled with individuals from their Apprenticeships, Internships and Spring Insight Programmes, creating a well-rounded junior talent journey at L'Oréal.

On the Management Trainee Programme, graduates work in functions across the business, gaining a sharp sense of life at L'Oréal. With three different rotations in their chosen stream, they're free to develop their talent and discover new possibilities. With on-the-job training and their own HR sponsor, graduates will progress into operational roles within as little as a year. They'll take on real responsibility, and make a palpable contribution to an international success story. From the start, they'll shape their own career; leading the change with L'Oréal's outstanding brands.

GRADUATE VACANCIES IN 2018
FINANCE
LOGISTICS
MARKETING
SALES

NUMBER OF VACANCIES
28 graduate jobs

LOCATIONS OF VACANCIES

STARTING SALARY FOR 2018
£30,000

UNIVERSITY VISITS IN 2017-18
ASTON, BATH, BIRMINGHAM, BRISTOL, DURHAM, EXETER, LANCASTER, LEEDS, LIVERPOOL, LONDON SCHOOL OF ECONOMICS, LOUGHBOROUGH, MANCHESTER, NEWCASTLE, NOTTINGHAM, NOTTINGHAM TRENT, UNIVERSITY COLLEGE LONDON, WARWICK, YORK
Please check with your university careers service for full details of local events.

MINIMUM ENTRY REQUIREMENTS
2.1 Degree

APPLICATION DEADLINE
Varies by function

FURTHER INFORMATION
www.Top100GraduateEmployers.com
Register now for the latest news, campus events, work experience and graduate vacancies at L'Oréal.

CAREERS.LOREAL.COM

GRADUATE VACANCIES IN 2018
GENERAL MANAGEMENT
LOGISTICS
PROPERTY
PURCHASING
RETAILING
SALES

NUMBER OF VACANCIES
250+ graduate jobs

LOCATIONS OF VACANCIES

STARTING SALARY FOR 2018
£36,000-£44,000

UNIVERSITY VISITS IN 2017-18
ASTON, BIRMINGHAM, BRISTOL, CARDIFF,
DURHAM, EDINBURGH, ESSEX, EXETER,
KENT, LEEDS, LIVERPOOL, MANCHESTER,
NORTHUMBRIA, NOTTINGHAM,
NOTTINGHAM TRENT, PLYMOUTH,
SOUTHAMPTON, SURREY, SWANSEA
*Please check with your university careers
service for full details of local events.*

MINIMUM ENTRY REQUIREMENTS
2.1 Degree

APPLICATION DEADLINE
Varies by function

FURTHER INFORMATION
www.Top100GraduateEmployers.com
*Register now for the latest news, campus
events, work experience and graduate
vacancies at Lidl.*

**Lidl are proud pioneers in the world of retail. With over 670
stores, 10 warehouses and 20,000 employees in the UK alone,
they're undoubtedly an established retailer. But it doesn't stop
there. With their recent expansion into the US and ambitious
plans for UK growth, they don't like to stand still.**

Continually challenging and changing the world of grocery retail, Lidl want to
make their stores, goods and shopping experience better than ever. And that's
where graduates come in.

Lidl is a brave and bright business and that's exactly what they're looking
for in their graduates. They're not looking for one type of person. They're
not looking for polished abilities and tonnes of experience. They're looking
for ambitious, committed people with personality and potential. Potential to
become one of the future leaders of the business. Each placement is individual
at Lidl. That's why their structured graduate programmes, award-winning
placement programme and countless graduate jobs, stretching across all areas
of the business, are all about giving students and graduates the opportunity to
develop. These graduates learn from the best retail managers and develop their
operational and management abilities from day one – and from there it's down
to the individual.

For those who are a born leader, everyday adventurer, hands-on hero or a
logistics legend, Lidl's graduate opportunities are all about pushing students and
graduates to make the most of their talent. So whether it's getting stuck in on
the rugby pitch and bringing their game whatever the weather, sorting out the
socials – and the logistics – at the SU, or stretching the budget and their creative
ability to feed a houseful on a fiver, Lidl are looking for that. That ability, that
talent, that potential, stands out from everyone else.

CLYM – LOGISTICS LEGEND

"IF I CAN TAKE A TEAM ACROSS THE ALPS ON BIKES, IMAGINE WHAT I CAN ACHIEVE IN STORE"

BRING YOUR BEST. WE'LL DO THE REST.

lidlgraduatecareers.co.uk

Linklaters

GRADUATE VACANCIES IN 2018

LAW

NUMBER OF VACANCIES
110 graduate jobs
For training contracts starting in 2020.

LOCATIONS OF VACANCIES

Vacancies also available in Europe, the USA, Asia and elsewhere in the world.

STARTING SALARY FOR 2018
£43,000

UNIVERSITY VISITS IN 2017-18
BELFAST, BIRMINGHAM, BRISTOL, CAMBRIDGE, DURHAM, EDINBURGH, EXETER, GLASGOW, KING'S COLLEGE LONDON, LEEDS, LEICESTER, LONDON SCHOOL OF ECONOMICS, MANCHESTER, NOTTINGHAM, OXFORD, QUEEN MARY LONDON, SCHOOL OF AFRICAN STUDIES, ST ANDREWS, TRINITY COLLEGE DUBLIN, UNIVERSITY COLLEGE DUBLIN, UNIVERSITY COLLEGE LONDON, WARWICK, YORK
Please check with your university careers service for full details of local events.

MINIMUM ENTRY REQUIREMENTS
2.1 Degree

APPLICATION DEADLINE
4th January 2018

FURTHER INFORMATION
www.Top100GraduateEmployers.com
Register now for the latest news, campus events, work experience and graduate vacancies at Linklaters.

From a shifting geopolitical landscape to the exponential growth in FinTech, this is a time of unprecedented change. Linklaters is ready. They go further to support clients, with market-leading legal insight and innovation. And they go further for each other, too.

When people join Linklaters, they find colleagues they want to work with. Inspiring, personable professionals who are generous with their time and always happy to help. Because to be best in class, Linklaters looks for open minded, team spirited individuals who will collaborate – and innovate – to deliver the smartest solutions for clients. Linklaters recruits candidates from a range of different backgrounds and disciplines, not just law. Why? Because those candidates bring with them a set of unique skills and perspectives that can help to challenge conventional thinking and inspire different approaches to client problems.

All Linklaters trainees benefit from pioneering learning and development opportunities, and an inclusive working culture that encourages them to fulfil their potential. Non-law graduates can take a one-year conversion course, the Graduate Diploma in Law. And all graduates complete the bespoke, accelerated Legal Practice Course before starting training contracts.

Then, over two years, trainees take four six-month seats (placements) in different practice areas and sometimes abroad. They work on high-profile deals across a global network of 29 offices, and gain the knowledge they need to qualify. And throughout their career, they enjoy the advantage of world-class training, courtesy of the Linklaters Law & Business School.

With their uniquely future-focused culture and high-profile, global opportunities, Linklaters provides the ideal preparation for a rewarding career, no matter what the future holds. Great change is here. Get ready.

Great change is here.

Linklaters

Are you ready?

From a shifting geopolitical landscape
to the exponential growth in FinTech,
this is a time of unprecedented change.

At Linklaters, we're ready. Our people
go further to support our clients,
with market-leading legal insight and
innovation. And we go further for each
other, too. We're people you want to work
with, generous with our time and ready
to help. So no matter what the future
holds, with us you'll be one step ahead.
Great change is here. Get ready.

Find out more at careers.linklaters.com

LLOYD'S

www.lloyds.com/graduates

facebook.com/lloyds **f**

linkedin.com/company/lloyd's-of-london **in**   twitter.com/LloydsofLondon **y**

Lloyd's is the foundation of the insurance industry and the future of it. Led by expert underwriters and brokers who cover more than 200 territories across the world, the Lloyd's market develops the complex insurance needed to empower human progress.

At Lloyd's, graduates help to make new endeavours possible, from space tourism to huge, groundbreaking events. They safeguard the world against risks from cyber terrorism to climate change. Above all, they'll help strengthen the resilience of local communities and drive global economic growth.

Lloyd's 24-month graduate schemes fall into two categories: functional schemes – including HR, IT, Finance and Marketing – and the Insurance scheme.

The Insurance scheme is the first graduate programme in the industry to be accredited by the Chartered Insurance Institute. On it, graduates will complete four different placements across the corporation and the market, giving them a 360° perspective of the specialist insurance industry. Whichever route is chosen, one thing's certain: graduates will gain a wealth of experience and benefit from comprehensive training. On the Insurance Graduate Scheme, graduates will gain the internationally recognised ACII qualification, while those on the functional schemes will work towards relevant postgraduate qualifications.

And all the while, exceptional employee benefits are on offer. These include not just a pension scheme, a competitive salary and 25 days' holiday a year, but also private medical insurance and a flexible benefits package.

With Lloyd's, graduates gain not just experience, technical training and qualifications, but also valuable soft skills like leadership and communication. In short, as they help to empower human progress, they will find that they progress fast too.

GRADUATE VACANCIES IN 2018

HUMAN RESOURCES

IT

LAW

MARKETING

NUMBER OF VACANCIES
10 graduate jobs

LOCATIONS OF VACANCIES

STARTING SALARY FOR 2018
£Competitive

UNIVERSITY VISITS IN 2018-19
KENT, MANCHESTER, QUEEN MARY LONDON, SOUTHAMPTON
Please check with your university careers service for full details of local events.

MINIMUM ENTRY REQUIREMENTS
2.2 Degree

APPLICATION DEADLINE
Varies by function
Early application advised.

FURTHER INFORMATION
www.Top100GraduateEmployers.com
Register now for the latest news, campus events, work experience and graduate vacancies at Lloyd's.

LLOYDS BANKING GROUP

www.lloydsbankinggrouptalent.com

twitter.com/LBGtalent 🐦   facebook.com/discoverwhatmatters **f**

instagram.com/LBGtalent 📷   linkedin.com/company/lloydsbankinggroup **in**

Lloyds Banking Group is a major UK financial services group with 320 years of history, providing trusted services to over 30 million UK customers, 13 million online users and 8 million mobile users through main brands such as Lloyds Bank, Halifax, Scottish Widows and Bank of Scotland.

The graduate opportunities at Lloyds Banking Group are as broad as the breadth and scale of their business. These include leading technology innovation, shaping strategy, and translating complex financial data, to helping high street customers, local businesses and global business clients. And with new technologies emerging and evolving, Lloyds Banking Group are looking for versatile, curious and courageous people to help lead the journey to becoming a financial organisation of the future. It's an incredible time to be part of this transforming industry.

Graduates and Interns are empowered to develop professionally and to embrace their passions and strengths – regardless of their degree, experiences or background. There are opportunities to gain professional qualifications, valuable insights and hands-on experience with teams and business leaders. Mentoring, workshops, training, volunteering activities and much more, ensure people can really discover just how far they can go.

At Lloyds Banking Group, all colleagues have something unique to offer, but they share a common purpose to help Britain prosper and make a positive difference to people, businesses and communities across the UK. There's a truly flexible and inclusive environment, which has been recognised in achievements such as inclusion in The Times Top 50 Employers for Women 2017. And there are as many opportunities to grow and learn from the variety of experiences of other new joiners, as there are from the diverse teams and people across the Group.

GRADUATE VACANCIES IN 2018

ACCOUNTANCY
CONSULTING
FINANCE
GENERAL MANAGEMENT
HUMAN RESOURCES
INVESTMENT BANKING
IT
LAW
SALES

NUMBER OF VACANCIES
300+ graduate jobs

LOCATIONS OF VACANCIES

STARTING SALARY FOR 2018
£28,000+
Plus relocation allowance, flex benefits and annual bonus.

UNIVERSITY VISITS IN 2017-18
ASTON, BATH, BIRMINGHAM, BRISTOL, CAMBRIDGE, CARDIFF, DURHAM, EDINBURGH, EXETER, GLASGOW, IMPERIAL COLLEGE LONDON, KING'S COLLEGE LONDON, KENT, LANCASTER, LEEDS, LEICESTER, LIVERPOOL, LONDON SCHOOL OF ECONOMICS, LOUGHBOROUGH, MANCHESTER, NOTTINGHAM, OXFORD, SHEFFIELD, SOUTHAMPTON, ST ANDREWS, STRATHCLYDE, UNIVERSITY COLLEGE LONDON, WARWICK
Please check with your university careers service for full details of local events.

MINIMUM ENTRY REQUIREMENTS
2.2 Degree

APPLICATION DEADLINE
31st December 2017

FURTHER INFORMATION
www.Top100GraduateEmployers.com
Register now for the latest news, campus events, work experience and graduate vacancies at Lloyds Banking Group.

LLOYDS BANKING GROUP

Bookworm

Movie buff

Data analyst

Organiser

"FIND YOUR STRENGTHS AND TAKE EVERY OPPORTUNITY TO FIND A CAREER THAT'S RIGHT FOR YOU."

MEERA, STRATEGY ACE

Bookworm and movie buff Meera likes a good story. Now she helps businesses build successful strategies by looking for stories and trends within their data. This is just one of the many career paths we offer through our Graduate Leadership Programme. Where will your strengths and passions take you?

CAREERS WORTH DISCOVERING

lloydsbankinggrouptalent.com

M&S

EST. 1884

M&S always strives for perfection. This passion to improve and meticulous attention to detail has led them to create products that millions of people love. Not to mention the on and offline experiences that push the boundaries for the entire retail industry and perfect careers for the talented people who work for them.

For ambitious graduates, there's no better place to begin their working life. Covering everything from Software Engineering and M&S Digital, to Retail Management, Marketing and beyond, each M&S graduate programme comes packed with unique opportunities for bright people to achieve the best for themselves and the business.

As an example, for those starting in Retail Management, the path to Commercial Manager level is clearly set out and, for many, achievable in as little as 9 months. But whichever part of the business a graduate joins, the day they start is the first step on a long and rewarding career with M&S – one where they'll be in an excellent position to achieve their potential as they help one of Britain's best-loved brands do the same.

It's truly an exciting time to be at M&S. With retail moving faster than ever before, anyone joining the company now will be building the business of the future. Whether it's spotting today's trends and turning them into tomorrow's reality, refining retail channels and enhancing shopping experiences or developing products and services on offer, it's all for the taking at M&S.

For graduates with high standards, a hard work ethic and an unwavering commitment to doing the right thing, a career at the forefront of retail awaits – along with a competitive salary and a host of other great benefits.

GRADUATE VACANCIES IN 2018

FINANCE
GENERAL MANAGEMENT
HUMAN RESOURCES
IT
LOGISTICS
MARKETING
PROPERTY
PURCHASING
RESEARCH & DEVELOPMENT
RETAILING

NUMBER OF VACANCIES
200 graduate jobs

LOCATIONS OF VACANCIES

STARTING SALARY FOR 2018
£23,500-£28,000

UNIVERSITY VISITS IN 2017-18
ASTON, BELFAST, BIRMINGHAM, CAMBRIDGE, CARDIFF, EDINBURGH, KENT, LEEDS, LEICESTER, LOUGHBOROUGH, NORTHUMBRIA, READING, SURREY, YORK
Please check with your university careers service for full details of local events.

MINIMUM ENTRY REQUIREMENTS
Dependent on scheme
Relevant degree required for some roles.

APPLICATION DEADLINE
Mid December 2017
Applications close earlier for some schemes – please see website for full details.

FURTHER INFORMATION
www.Top100GraduateEmployers.com
Register now for the latest news, campus events, work experience and graduate vacancies at M&S.

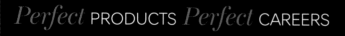

MARS

big. start.

MARS | grow beyond.

GRADUATE VACANCIES IN 2018
ENGINEERING
FINANCE
GENERAL MANAGEMENT
HUMAN RESOURCES
IT
LOGISTICS
MARKETING
PURCHASING
RESEARCH & DEVELOPMENT
SALES

NUMBER OF VACANCIES
35-40 graduate jobs

LOCATIONS OF VACANCIES

Vacancies also available in Europe.

STARTING SALARY FOR 2018
Up to £32,000
Plus a £2,000 joining bonus.

UNIVERSITY VISITS IN 2017-18
BATH, BIRMINGHAM, CAMBRIDGE,
DURHAM, EXETER, LEEDS, NOTTINGHAM,
OXFORD, WARWICK
*Please check with your university careers
service for full details of local events.*

MINIMUM ENTRY REQUIREMENTS
2.1 Degree
280-300 UCAS points

APPLICATION DEADLINE
30th November 2017

FURTHER INFORMATION
www.Top100GraduateEmployers.com
*Register now for the latest news, campus
events, work experience and graduate
vacancies at Mars.*

Think Maltesers®, M&Ms®, Uncle Ben's®, Pedigree®, Whiskas®, Extra® and Orbit®, some of the nation's best-loved and well-known brands. Think the world's third-largest food company with international operations in 370 locations. Know what makes Mars special? Think again.

Sure, Mars is one of the world's leading food companies, but it's more like a community than a corporate. Because it's still a private, family-owned business with a Mars family of 80,000 associates across the world. Associates at Mars are united and guided by The Five Principles – Quality, Responsibility, Mutuality, Efficiency and Freedom. These are key to the culture and help associates to make business decisions they are proud of.

The culture at Mars is relationship driven – and it's how these relationships are built that's most important. Collaborating with others is key to getting things done. Mars encourages open communication as this builds relationships of trust and respect.

Mars want to stretch and challenge Associates every day to help them reach their full potential. So they take learning and development seriously – it makes good business sense for Mars to have people performing at the top of their game. With great managers, mentors and peers, graduates and students will be supported the whole way. And they will support other associates on their journey too.

At Mars, graduates and students are offered an unrivalled opportunity to make a difference in their roles from day one. Mars wants everything they do to matter and wants their work to make a positive difference to customers, suppliers, associates and the world we live in. Graduates will have endless support to develop both personally and professionally, creating a start to an exciting and fulfilling career at Mars.

start. here.

today a graduate. tomorrow a leader.

Our graduate development programmes are different to most.

You'll be put into a role with big responsibility right from day one - we offer real freedom here and you'll know how to make the most of it. For one thing, we don't have a set way of working. If you think we can do things better or more efficiently, we want you to let us know. And that's not all. It will be very much down to you to seek out new opportunities – new opportunities for our business, for your projects and for your career.

We think that's far more rewarding than being spoon-fed or told what to do and when. And doing so can help you grow beyond your current aspirations enabling you to develop at a considerable pace. Rise to the challenges, and before you know it, you'll be stepping up to a leadership role. What this means is that you'll need to be full of drive and ambition. You certainly won't be afraid of responsibility – in fact, you're the kind of person who craves it.

Full of initiative and a top-notch communicator, you won't just come up with ideas, you'll find ways to make them happen. And because this is an open, collaborative culture where there is a huge importance placed on building relationships, you'll be as happy listening to the ideas of others as you are sharing your own. You'll be warm and friendly in your approach and you'll actively seek out contacts rather than waiting for people to come to you. At Mars, the way you engage and interact with others is paramount to our success.

We ask for a lot. But we don't think there's a more exciting place to start and grow your career **– and in terms of how far you can progress and how fast, the future is wide open.**

MARS.CO.UK/CAREERS

Follow us on social media:

Facebook – Mars Graduates & Students
Twitter – @MarsGradsUK

MARS | grow beyond.

whiskas Extra Twix

GRADUATE VACANCIES IN 2018
GENERAL MANAGEMENT

NUMBER OF VACANCIES
50 graduate jobs

LOCATIONS OF VACANCIES

McDonald's has operated in the UK since 1974 and and the business is growing consistently with our 1,270 restaurants and over 110,000 employees. It is the biggest family restaurant business in the world, serving approximately 3.7 million customers a day in the UK alone.

Training and developing people has been at the heart of the McDonald's business throughout its 42 years in the UK. Each year the company invests over £40 million in developing its people and providing opportunities for progression. Attracting, retaining and engaging the best people is key to their business.

It has a proven track record of career progression and prospective managers can create a long-term career with one of the world's most recognised and successful brands.

A graduate job at McDonald's is focused on restaurant management – it involves overseeing the performance and development of an average of 80 employees and identifying ways in which to improve customer service, build sales and profitability. Following the training period, which can last up to six months, Trainee Managers are promoted to Assistant Managers and become part of the core restaurant management team. Successful Trainee Managers can, in future, progress to managing all aspects of a £multi million business – opportunities can then arise to progress to area management roles or secondments in support departments. Trainee Managers need to be logical thinkers, have a great attitude and be committed to delivering a great customer experience.

Working for a progressive company has its perks – including a host of benefits such as a quarterly bonus scheme, six weeks holiday allowance, meal allowance, private healthcare and access to discounts at hundreds of retailers.

STARTING SALARY FOR 2018
£22,000

UNIVERSITY VISITS IN 2017-18
Please check with your university careers service for full details of local events.

APPLICATION DEADLINE
Year-round recruitment

FURTHER INFORMATION
www.Top100GraduateEmployers.com
Register now for the latest news, campus events, work experience and graduate vacancies at McDonald's.

SETTING MYSELF UP FOR THE FUTURE

With McDonald's, I can.

Our Trainee Manager Programme is the first step to managing a £multi-million restaurant employing 80 staff.

After six months of training and learning the basics, our Trainee Managers are promoted to Assistant Managers – but if you've got the drive and ambition, there's no limit to how far you can go.

To find out more about working and learning with us visit

people.mcdonalds.co.uk

McKinsey&Company

McKinsey & Company helps world-leading clients in the public, private and third sectors to meet their biggest strategic, operational and organisational challenges. Their goal is to provide distinctive and long-lasting performance improvements – in short, it is about having an impact. Making a difference.

As a consultant in this truly global firm, graduates will have the opportunity to work with colleagues and clients from all around the world. They will come into contact with CEOs, government leaders and the foremost charitable organisations, and work together with them on their most exciting and challenging issues.

Working as part of a small team, and dedicated to one project at a time, graduates will be fully involved from the very start of their first project. No two weeks will be the same: from gathering and analysing data, to interviewing stakeholders or presenting findings to clients, the range of industries and business issues to which successful applicants have exposure will mean that they are constantly acquiring new skills and experience. Bright, motivated newcomers can expect their ideas and opinions to be encouraged and valued, right from day one.

Graduates will also enjoy world-class personal and professional development. Formal training programmes, coupled with a culture of mentoring and coaching, will provide the best possible support.

Working in consulting is challenging, but McKinsey encourages a healthy work-life balance. Successful applicants will find like-minded individuals, and a thriving range of groups, initiatives and events that bring people together.

McKinsey & Company is welcoming applications for both full time and summer internship applications.

GRADUATE VACANCIES IN 2018
CONSULTING

NUMBER OF VACANCIES
No fixed quota

LOCATIONS OF VACANCIES

Vacancies also available elsewhere in the world.

STARTING SALARY FOR 2018
£Competitive

UNIVERSITY VISITS IN 2017-18
BATH, BIRMINGHAM, BRISTOL, CAMBRIDGE, DURHAM, EDINBURGH, EXETER, IMPERIAL COLLEGE LONDON, LEEDS, LONDON SCHOOL OF ECONOMICS, MANCHESTER, NOTTINGHAM, OXFORD, ST ANDREWS, TRINITY COLLEGE DUBLIN, UNIVERSITY COLLEGE DUBLIN, UNIVERSITY COLLEGE LONDON, WARWICK
Please check with your university careers service for full details of local events.

MINIMUM ENTRY REQUIREMENTS
2.1 Degree

APPLICATION DEADLINE
26th October 2017

FURTHER INFORMATION
www.Top100GraduateEmployers.com
Register now for the latest news, campus events, work experience and graduate vacancies at McKinsey & Company.

Don't just come to work. Come to change.

We welcome applications from all degree disciplines.

Deadline dates:

Full time opportunities 26 October 2017

Internship opportunities 25 January 2018

www.mckinsey.com/careers
www.facebook.com/McKinseyCareersUKIreland

MI5 helps safeguard the UK against threats to national security including terrorism and espionage. It investigates suspect individuals and organisations to gather intelligence relating to security threats. MI5 also advises the critical national infrastructure on protective security measures, to help them reduce their vulnerability.

Graduates from a range of backgrounds join MI5 for stimulating and rewarding careers, in a supportive environment, whilst enjoying a good work-life balance. Many graduates join the Intelligence Officer Development Programme, which is a structured 3-5 year programme designed to teach new joiners about MI5 investigations and give them the skills to run them. After completing one post of two years or two posts of one year in areas which teach aspects of investigative work, and subject to successful completion of its Foundation Investigative Training (FIT), graduates will then take up an investigative post as a fully trained Intelligence Officer. There will be opportunities to move to new roles and experience new challenges every 2-3 years.

MI5 also deals with vast amounts of data and interpreting that data is vital to its intelligence work. The Intelligence and Data Analyst Development Programme is a structured two-year programme which prepares graduates to be part of this specialist career stream. It will take new joiners from the basics through to the most advanced data analytical techniques. As they progress they will be able to work in different teams across the range of MI5's investigations using analytical expertise to make a direct impact on keeping the country safe.

MI5 also offers a Technology Graduate Development Programme which is a structured programme that gives graduates the experience, knowledge and skills they need to be an effective technology professional in its pioneering IT function.

GRADUATE VACANCIES IN 2018
GENERAL MANAGEMENT
IT

NUMBER OF VACANCIES
150 graduate jobs

LOCATIONS OF VACANCIES

STARTING SALARY FOR 2018
£30,000+

UNIVERSITY VISITS IN 2017-18
Please check with your university careers service for full details of local events.

MINIMUM ENTRY REQUIREMENTS
2.2 Degree

APPLICATION DEADLINE
Varies by function

FURTHER INFORMATION
www.Top100GraduateEmployers.com
Register now for the latest news, campus events, work experience and graduate vacancies at MI5.

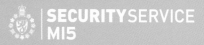

"I NEVER THOUGHT MY SKILLS COULD HELP PROTECT A NATION"

The future is in your hands.

At MI5 everyone has one thing in common – a commitment to protecting the UK from serious threats. This requires people from a variety of cultures and backgrounds with a range of experiences, who can bring different perspectives to our work. Join us and you'll enjoy the chance to develop your skills in a supportive environment and help keep the country safe. Find out how you'll fit in at www.mi5.gov.uk/careers

To apply to MI5 you must be a born or naturalised British citizen, over 18 years old and normally have lived in the UK for nine of the last ten years. You should not discuss your application, other than with your partner or a close family member, providing that they are British. They should also be made aware of the importance of discretion.

disability confident

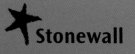

Stonewall

Morgan Stanley

Morgan Stanley is one of the world's leading financial services firms. They generate, manage and distribute capital, helping businesses get the funds they need to develop innovative products and services that benefit millions. Their work is defined by the passion and dedication of their people, and their goals are achieved through hiring, training and rewarding the best possible talent.

At Morgan Stanley attitude is just as important as aptitude, and they want to work with and develop students and graduates who show integrity and commitment to their core values, who share their commitment to providing first-class client service, and who embrace change and innovation. Because the firm values a diversity of perspectives it encourages people to be themselves and pursue their own interests.

There are numerous opportunities to learn and grow professionally and help put the power of capital to work. All of Morgan Stanley's programmes are designed to provide the knowledge and toolkit graduates need to develop quickly into an effective and successful professional in their chosen area. Training is not limited to the first weeks or months on the job but continues throughout a graduate's career. Over time, they could become part of the next generation of leaders, and play a part in technological, scientific and cultural advancements that change the world forever.

Morgan Stanley believes that capital can work to benefit all. This success needs financial capital, but its foundation is intellectual capital. The talents and points of view of the diverse individuals working for them helps to build their legacy and shape their future. This is why Morgan Stanley accept applicants from all degree disciplines who demonstrate academic excellence.

GRADUATE VACANCIES IN 2018

FINANCE
HUMAN RESOURCES
INVESTMENT BANKING
IT

NUMBER OF VACANCIES
200+ graduate jobs

LOCATIONS OF VACANCIES

Vacancies also available in Europe.

STARTING SALARY FOR 2018
£Competitive
Plus benefits and a discretionary bonus.

UNIVERSITY VISITS IN 2017-18
Please check with your university careers service for full details of local events.

MINIMUM ENTRY REQUIREMENTS
2.1 Degree

APPLICATION DEADLINE
Varies by function

FURTHER INFORMATION
www.Top100GraduateEmployers.com
*Register now for the latest news, campus events, work experience and graduate vacancies at **Morgan Stanley**.*

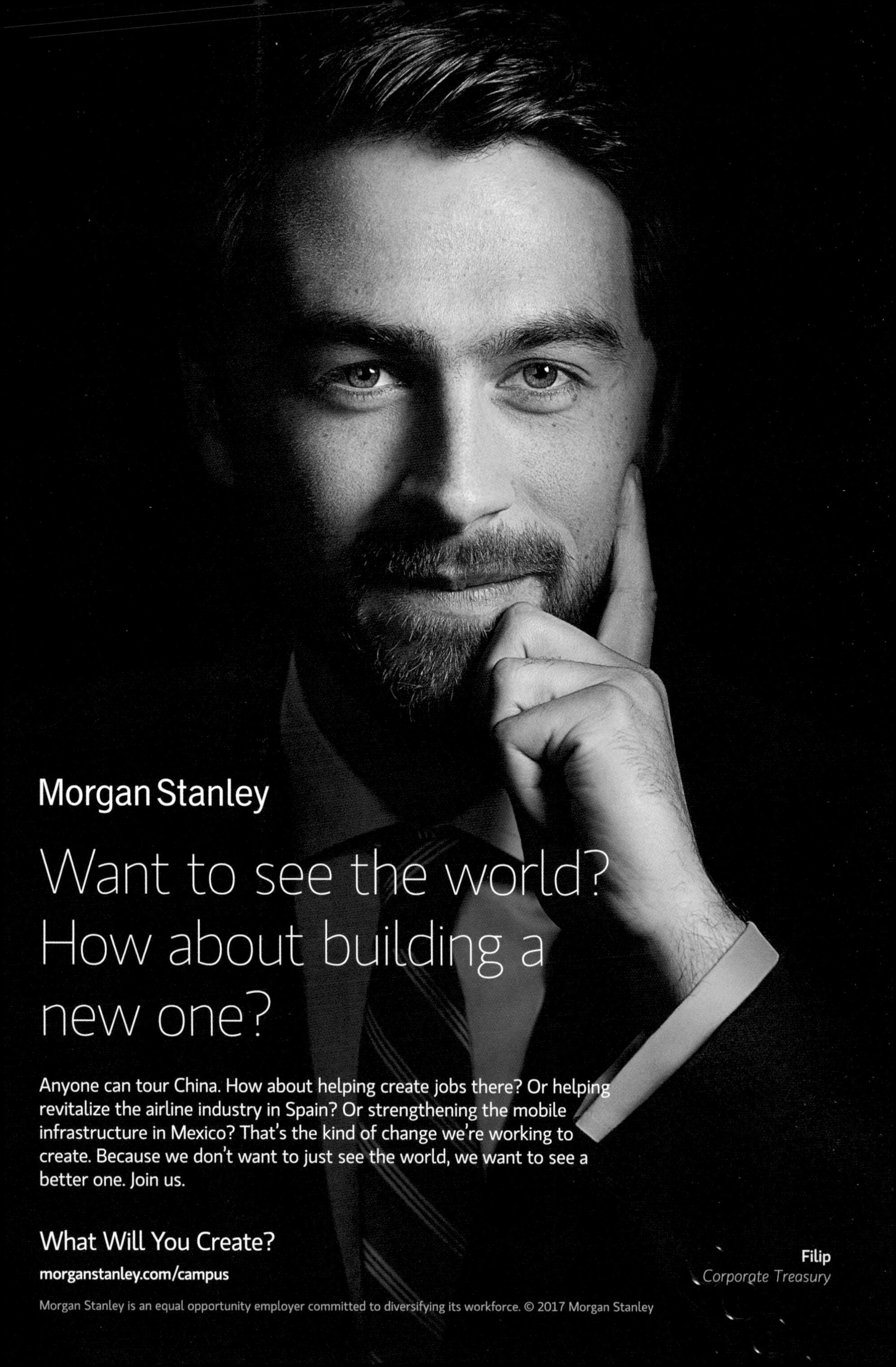
Morgan Stanley
Want to see the world? How about building a new one?
Anyone can tour China. How about helping create jobs there? Or helping revitalize the airline industry in Spain? Or strengthening the mobile infrastructure in Mexico? That's the kind of change we're working to create. Because we don't want to just see the world, we want to see a better one. Join us.
What Will You Create?
morganstanley.com/campus
Morgan Stanley is an equal opportunity employer committed to diversifying its workforce. © 2017 Morgan Stanley
Filip
Corporate Treasury

GRADUATE VACANCIES IN 2018

CONSULTING

ENGINEERING

PROPERTY

NUMBER OF VACANCIES
250 graduate jobs

LOCATIONS OF VACANCIES

Mott MacDonald is a global engineering, management and development consultancy focused on guiding clients through many of the planet's most intricate challenges. By challenging norms and unlocking creativity, Mott MacDonald delivers long-lasting value for societies around the globe.

Improvement is at the heart of what Mott MacDonald offers. Better economic development, better social and environmental outcomes, better businesses and a better return on investment. Their 16,000-strong network of experts are joined-up across sectors and geographies, giving their graduates access to an exceptional breadth and depth of expertise and experience, enhancing their knowledge with the right support and guidance every step of the way. The consultancy's employees, active in 150 countries, take leading roles on some of the world's highest profile projects, turning obstacles into elegant, sustainable solutions. Individuals who get satisfaction from working on projects that benefit communities around the world will thrive at Mott MacDonald. Additionally, as Mott MacDonald is an employee-owned company it allows them to choose the work they take on and focus on the issues that are important.

Mott MacDonald's graduate schemes are more than just a standard graduate job. With the help of a dedicated learning and development team, the accredited schemes aim to give graduates the opportunity to continually progress and develop in their chosen field. The schemes have been created specifically to enable graduates to be the best that they can be. All entry level professionals are enrolled into the Mott MacDonald Academy, a structured development programme introducing key business and commercial competencies.

Connect to opportunity at Mott MacDonald.

STARTING SALARY FOR 2018
£25,000-£28,000

UNIVERSITY VISITS IN 2017-18
BATH, BIRMINGHAM, BRISTOL, CAMBRIDGE, CARDIFF, DURHAM, EDINBURGH, GLASGOW, HERIOT-WATT, IMPERIAL COLLEGE LONDON, LEEDS, LIVERPOOL, MANCHESTER, NEWCASTLE, OXFORD, PLYMOUTH, READING, SHEFFIELD, SOUTHAMPTON, STRATHCLYDE, WARWICK
Please check with your university careers service for full details of local events.

MINIMUM ENTRY REQUIREMENTS
2.1 Degree

APPLICATION DEADLINE
13th November 2017

FURTHER INFORMATION
www.Top100GraduateEmployers.com
Register now for the latest news, campus events, work experience and graduate vacancies at Mott MacDonald.

MOTT
MACDONALD

Unlocking creativity

Be part of a dedicated team delivering
long-lasting value at every stage of a project.
Working in all areas of infrastructure,
management and development, we look
at challenges from a fresh angle, creating
solutions that improve people's lives.

We are Mott MacDonald.
We open opportunities with connected thinking.

mottmac.com/careers/graduate

www.nestleacademy.co.uk

twitter.com/nestleacademy 𝕐 facebook.com/Nestle.Academy.Careers f

instagram.com/nestle_academy 🅞 linkedin.com/company/nestle-s-a- in

As the world's largest food and drink manufacturer, people will definitely have come across Nestlé before. Nescafé, Kit Kat and Shredded Wheat are just some of their household names. Not to mention Buxton natural mineral water, Felix cat food and Rowntree's Fruit Pastilles.

But behind all the world-famous brands, there are lots of other things that Nestlé does that people might not be so familiar with.

For example, their research is pushing back the boundaries of health and nutrition. Nestlé want to help shape a better and healthier world, and inspire people to live healthier lives. They have offices, factories and plants not just across the UK but throughout Europe and around the world. In fact, across 86 countries they employ over 330,000 people.

Joining Nestlé gives graduates the opportunity not only to work on their successful brands, but also to explore this hugely diverse and complex organisation by moving through different roles, different teams and different business areas. A graduate career with Nestlé will have a local emphasis as well as a potential global reach.

And thanks to the world-class learning and development offered by the Nestlé Academy, successful applicants will be able to build on their existing strengths to become a highly skilled and experienced expert in their field. The Academy provides a variety of career development routes throughout the organisation including on the job training, providing graduates the opportunities for continuous improvement at every stage of their career.

Graduates at Nestlé will need to demonstrate their commercial understanding, their ability to work with and lead other people, and have the confidence to take the initiative and stand by their decisions.

GRADUATE VACANCIES IN 2018

ENGINEERING
FINANCE
HUMAN RESOURCES
LOGISTICS
MARKETING
SALES

NUMBER OF VACANCIES
25 graduate jobs

LOCATIONS OF VACANCIES

STARTING SALARY FOR 2018
£27,000
Plus a £2,000 joining bonus.

UNIVERSITY VISITS IN 2017-18
EDINBURGH, GLASGOW, KING'S COLLEGE LONDON, LEEDS, MANCHESTER, NEWCASTLE, NORTHUMBRIA, UNIVERSITY COLLEGE LONDON, YORK
Please check with your university careers service for full details of local events.

APPLICATION DEADLINE
Varies by function

FURTHER INFORMATION
www.Top100GraduateEmployers.com
Register now for the latest news, campus events, work experience and graduate vacancies at Nestlé.

Network Rail own and operate the railway infrastructure in England, Scotland and Wales. Their purpose is to create a better railway for a better Britain. It is the fastest growing and safest rail network in Europe, presenting an abundance of opportunities for ambitious and enthusiastic graduates.

Network Rail have £25bn earmarked to invest in landmark projects and initiatives as part of their Railway Upgrade Plan. They are already making history through some of the largest engineering projects in Europe: Crossrail, Birmingham New Street Station, London Bridge, HS2 and Thameslink.

Although Rail is a huge part of their business, they are also one of the largest land and property owners in Britain. They manage a portfolio that includes 18 of the biggest stations in Britain, the retail outlets inside them and the small businesses that live under their arches.

Network Rail are looking to invest in graduates who are committed to making a difference, to help transform Britain's rail infrastructure, transport network and economy for the 22nd century.

They have supported thousands of graduates through their diverse and challenging programmes. Graduates will have access to Westwood, their state-of-the-art training centre in Coventry, and six other training facilities.

There are two entry routes for graduates. Within Engineering there are three specific schemes: Civil, Electrical and Electronic and Mechanical engineering.

In Business Management, applicants can choose from the following schemes: Finance, General Management, Health, Safety and Environment, HR, IT & Business Services, Project Management, Property and Supply Chain Management.

There are also summer and year in industry placements available for those who would like to find out what it is like to work for Network Rail before graduation.

GRADUATE VACANCIES IN 2018

ENGINEERING
FINANCE
GENERAL MANAGEMENT
HUMAN RESOURCES
IT
LOGISTICS
PROPERTY
PURCHASING

NUMBER OF VACANCIES
Around 175 graduate jobs

LOCATIONS OF VACANCIES

STARTING SALARY FOR 2018
£26,500

UNIVERSITY VISITS IN 2017-18
BIRMINGHAM, BRUNEL, CARDIFF, CITY, DUNDEE, DURHAM, EDINBURGH, GLASGOW, IMPERIAL COLLEGE LONDON, LEEDS, LEICESTER, LOUGHBOROUGH, MANCHESTER, NEWCASTLE, NORTHUMBRIA, NOTTINGHAM, OXFORD BROOKES, READING, SHEFFIELD, STRATHCLYDE, UNIVERSITY COLLEGE LONDON
Please check with your university careers service for full details of local events.

MINIMUM ENTRY REQUIREMENTS
2.2 Degree

APPLICATION DEADLINE
December 2017

FURTHER INFORMATION
www.Top100GraduateEmployers.com
Register now for the latest news, campus events, work experience and graduate vacancies at Network Rail.

NetworkRail

The difference is you

Standout graduate and placement opportunities at Network Rail

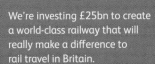

We're investing £25bn to create a world-class railway that will really make a difference to rail travel in Britain.

We need you to help turn our plans into reality.

— Are you ready for a career as bright and unique as you are?

Opportunities available in:

Engineering
– Civil engineering
– Electrical & electronic engineering
– Mechanical engineering

Business management
– Finance
– General management
– Health, safety & environment
– Human resources
– IT & business services
– Project management
– Property
– Supply Chain management

Find out more at
networkrail.co.uk/graduates

NEWTON

THIS IS YOU
TO THE N^{TH} DEGREE

Experience it at **newtoneurope.com/spirit**

Newton isn't like most consultancies. Their business model is purposefully disruptive. They hire people with spirit, personality and bravery – and go to extraordinary lengths to build their skills and belief. They also offer unusual levels of responsibility.

When asked "Why Newton?" the three top reasons people give are: a vibrant culture that's characterised by a strong sense of fellowship; its 'get-stuck-right-in' working style; and its unmatched record of producing up to 50% improvement in six months for their clients, without capital expenditure.

Newton has so much belief in the quality of their consultants' solutions, they put 100% of their fees at risk to deliver guaranteed results. It's a radical model, one that's helped transform organisations that set global agendas, and services that support entire communities. It's also won them numerous awards across the public and private sectors, from health and social care to defence, grocery, manufacturing, transport and utilities.

To make this type of promise, it takes a team that knows how to be different. Newton people aren't tied to the office or submerged in paperwork; they're given the means and skills to work alongside client teams, bring about visible change, and get results that are not only sustainable but actually make a difference in the world. They're also given the scope to accelerate their own personal and professional development: from grass roots to management and beyond.

Newton's philosophy is simple: they demand better – not just for their clients but for their people. It's a place where initiative, creativity and versatility thrive. Where consultants aren't just colleagues; they're friends who inspire, challenge and support each other. It is a consultancy where, if graduates don't limit themselves, nothing will limit them.

Careers in Consulting
SPIRIT
TO THE NTH DEGREE
If you approach a challenge with a grin not a grimace; if your neurons spark into life as the odds mount against you; if you'd flourish in a community of minds as sharp, as challenging and as open as yours – well, we have a consulting career with your name on it. Take your potential to the nth degree at **newtoneurope.com/spirit**
NEWTON

NATIONAL GRADUATE
DEVELOPMENT PROGRAMME
ngdp
FOR LOCAL GOVERNMENT

www.ngdp.org.uk

ngdp@local.gov.uk

twitter.com/ngdp_LGA   facebook.com/NGDPLGA

The ngdp is a two-year graduate development programme which gives committed graduates the opportunity and training to make a positive difference in local communities. Run by the Local Government Association, the ngdp is looking to equip the sector's next generation of high-calibre managers.

Local government is the largest and most diverse employer in the UK, with around 1.2 million staff based in 375 local authorities and in excess of 500 different occupational areas. More than 1,200 graduates have completed the ngdp since 1999 and gained access to rewarding careers in and beyond the sector, with many currently holding influential managerial and policy roles.

In the midst of the huge changes taking place within the public sector, ngdp graduates are positioned to make a real contribution to shaping and implementing new ideas and initiatives from day one. Graduate trainees are employed by a participating council (or group of councils) for a minimum of two years, during which time they rotate between a series of placements in key areas of the council. Trainees can experience a range of roles in strategy, front-line service and support to expand their perspective of local government's many different capacities and gain a flexible, transferable skill set.

ngdp graduates also benefit from being part of a national cohort of like-minded peers. Together they will participate in a national induction event, join an established knowledge-sharing network and gain a post-graduate qualification in Leadership and Management. The learning and development programme gives graduates the chance to learn from established professionals and also each other.

The ngdp has been enabling graduates to build varied and rewarding careers for almost twenty years. Join now to start working in an exciting period of opportunity and change for the benefit of local communities.

GRADUATE VACANCIES IN 2018
ACCOUNTANCY
FINANCE
GENERAL MANAGEMENT
HUMAN RESOURCES
IT
LAW
MEDIA
PROPERTY
PURCHASING
RESEARCH & DEVELOPMENT

NUMBER OF VACANCIES
Over 150 graduate jobs

LOCATIONS OF VACANCIES

STARTING SALARY FOR 2018
£24,174+
Excluding inner and outer London weighting where appropriate.

UNIVERSITY VISITS IN 2017-18
BATH, BIRMINGHAM, BRISTOL, BRUNEL, CAMBRIDGE, CARDIFF, CITY, DURHAM, EAST ANGLIA, ESSEX, EXETER, IMPERIAL COLLEGE LONDON, KEELE, KING'S COLLEGE LONDON, LANCASTER, LEEDS, LEICESTER, LIVERPOOL, LONDON SCHOOL OF ECONOMICS, LOUGHBOROUGH, MANCHESTER, NEWCASTLE, NORTHUMBRIA, NOTTINGHAM, NOTTINGHAM TRENT, OXFORD, PLYMOUTH, QUEEN MARY LONDON, READING, ROYAL HOLLOWAY, SHEFFIELD, UNIVERSITY COLLEGE LONDON, WARWICK, YORK
Please check with your university careers service for full details of local events.

MINIMUM ENTRY REQUIREMENTS
2.2 Degree

APPLICATION DEADLINE
4th January 2018

FURTHER INFORMATION
www.Top100GraduateEmployers.com
Register now for the latest news, campus events, work experience and graduate vacancies at **Local Government***.*

**Housing. Social Care.
Public Health. Education.**

The national graduate development programme for local government is a two year programme focussing on local government's biggest challenges. Providing work experience placements across a range of different departments and a national post graduate qualification, the scheme will provide you with unparalleled opportunities for personal and professional development.

"The NGDP has given me an invaluable opportunity to achieve what I have always wanted to do: take real responsibility for creating real change in local government while helping local communities."

**Jennifer McErlain
Oldham Council**

Real life. Real work.
Your opportunity to
make a difference.

**Start your career in local government.
Find out more at: www.ngdp.org.uk**

@ngdp_LGA I #ngdp20

www.facebook.com/NGDPLGA

NHS
Leadership Academy

Graduate Management
Training Scheme

A DAY IN THEATRE
TAUGHT ME
ABOUT TEAMWORK

As Europe's largest employer with an annual budget of over £100billion, there is no other organisation on Earth quite like the NHS. And with the ability to have a positive impact on over 53 million people, the NHS Graduate Management Training Scheme really is nothing less than a life-defining experience.

It's unquestionably hard work, but this multi-award-winning, fast-track development scheme, enables graduates to become the healthcare leaders of the future.

Graduates specialise in one of six areas: Finance, General Management, Human Resources, Health Informatics, Policy and Strategy, and Health Analysis. As they grow personally and professionally they'll gain specialist skills while receiving full support from a dedicated mentor at Executive level.

Everyone joining the scheme will experience a comprehensive learning & development package designed by some of the most experienced and expert learning providers in the UK.

Success is granted only to those who are prepared to give their heart and soul to their profession. The responsibility of the NHS demands that their future leaders have the tenacity, the focus, and the determination to deliver nothing but the best.

Because the scheme offers a fast-track route to a senior-level role, graduates will soon find themselves facing complex problems head on and tackling high-profile situations. Working for the NHS means standing up to high levels of public scrutiny and having decisions closely inspected. Graduates who want to succeed will need to be thick-skinned, resilient and able to respond to constant change.

This is a career where the hard work and unfaltering commitment of graduates not only affects the lives of others, but it will ultimately define their own.

GRADUATE VACANCIES IN 2018
ACCOUNTANCY
FINANCE
GENERAL MANAGEMENT
HUMAN RESOURCES
IT
RESEARCH & DEVELOPMENT

NUMBER OF VACANCIES
200 graduate jobs

LOCATIONS OF VACANCIES

STARTING SALARY FOR 2018
£23,000
Plus location allowance where appropriate.

UNIVERSITY VISITS IN 2017-18
Please check with your university careers service for full details of local events.

MINIMUM ENTRY REQUIREMENTS
2.2 Degree

APPLICATION DEADLINE
December 2017

FURTHER INFORMATION
www.Top100GraduateEmployers.com
Register now for the latest news, campus events, work experience and graduate vacancies at the NHS.

WHEN I BECAME A
MANAGER
IN THE
CARDIOVASCULAR
DIVISION,
I REALISED I WAS HELPING THE NATION BEAT HEART DISEASE.
THIS IS NO ORDINARY GRADUATE SCHEME.

The NHS Graduate Management Training Scheme is nothing less than a life defining experience. Whether you join our Finance, General Management, Human Resources, Health Analysis, Health Informatics, or Policy and Strategy scheme, you'll receive everything you need to make a positive impact on the lives of 53 million people across England.

These aren't clinical opportunities, but this is about developing exceptional healthcare leaders. High-calibre management professionals who will lead the NHS through a profound transformation and shape our services around ever-evolving patient needs. Inspirational people who will push up standards, deliver deeper value for money and continue the drive towards a healthier nation.

nhsgraduates.co.uk

Life Defining

NHS
Leadership Academy

Graduate Management
Training Scheme

graduate.recruitment@nortonrosefulbright.com

twitter.com/NLawGrad   facebook.com/NortonRoseFulbrightGraduatesUK

@NLawGrad   instagram.com/nortonrosefulbright

NORTON ROSE FULBRIGHT

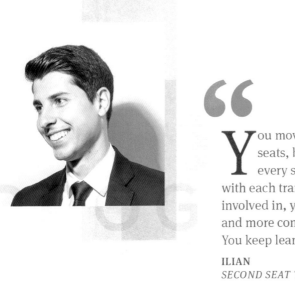

"You move through seats, but I think with every step you take, with each transaction you're involved in, you get more and more comfortable. You keep learning."

ILIAN
SECOND SEAT TRAINEE

Norton Rose Fulbright is a global law firm. It provides the world's preeminent corporations and financial institutions with a full business law service. The practice has more than 4,000 lawyers and other legal staff based in over 50 cities worldwide.

Recognised for its industry focus, the practice is strong across all the key sectors: financial institutions; energy; infrastructure, mining and commodities; transport; technology and innovation; and life sciences and healthcare.

Norton Rose Fulbright recruits up to 50 trainee solicitors each year. Its training contract is based on a four-seat pattern, allowing trainees to gain the widest possible exposure to different practice areas and offices around the world. Trainees have the opportunity to spend at least one of their seats on an international or client secondment, in addition to seats in Corporate, Banking and Litigation, enabling them to make the best and most informed choice of qualification.

Each year, Norton Rose Fulbright runs three vacation schemes for law and non-law applicants which are designed to provide an invaluable insight into life and work inside a global legal practice. Successful applicants will have the opportunity to participate in actual work with clients – which could involve anything from legal research to attending meetings or court. Students will also attend training sessions, breakfast briefings about Norton Rose Fulbright's practice areas and social events with current trainees, lawyers, and partners.

Norton Rose Fulbright also run open days throughout the year for penultimate-year undergraduates, finalists and graduates, as well as a first step programme for first-year undergraduates.

GRADUATE VACANCIES IN 2018
LAW

NUMBER OF VACANCIES
45 graduate jobs
For training contracts starting in 2020.

LOCATIONS OF VACANCIES

STARTING SALARY FOR 2018
£44,000

UNIVERSITY VISITS IN 2017-18
BIRMINGHAM, BRISTOL, CAMBRIDGE, DURHAM, EXETER, KING'S COLLEGE LONDON, LEEDS, LONDON SCHOOL OF ECONOMICS, MANCHESTER, NEWCASTLE, NOTTINGHAM, OXFORD, QUEEN MARY LONDON, UNIVERSITY COLLEGE LONDON, WARWICK, YORK
Please check with your university careers service for full details of local events.

MINIMUM ENTRY REQUIREMENTS
2.1 Degree
340 UCAS points

APPLICATION DEADLINE
Year-round recruitment
Early application advised.

FURTHER INFORMATION
www.Top100GraduateEmployers.com
Register now for the latest news, campus events, work experience and graduate vacancies at Norton Rose Fulbright.

NORTON ROSE FULBRIGHT

PROGRESS

WITH PURPOSE

How do you know when you're making progress? It's all about the firsts. First day. First client. First deal closed. First mistake, and what you learned from it. It's the little steps as well as the big ones. And here's one for you now: first encounter with your future. Find out about our training contracts and vacation schemes at nortonrosefulbrightgraduates.com

www.oxfam.org.uk
internships@oxfam.org.uk

GRADUATE VACANCIES IN 2018
ACCOUNTANCY
HUMAN RESOURCES
IT
MARKETING
MEDIA
RESEARCH & DEVELOPMENT
RETAILING

NUMBER OF VACANCIES
50+ Voluntary internships

LOCATIONS OF VACANCIES

Oxfam is a global movement of people who won't live with poverty. For more than 70 years, they've saved and rebuilt lives in disasters, helped people build better lives, and spoken out on the issues that keep people poor. Right now they're helping people in more than 90 countries worldwide.

For the last ten years, Oxfam's voluntary internship scheme has helped provide valuable experience and skills to hundreds of people. They offer structured roles based around an individual's abilities and interests – usually for one to three days a week, for a period of three to seven months. Local travel and lunch expenses are covered to ensure no one is out of pocket while volunteering.

An Oxfam intern will have the unique advantage of joining some of the world's most passionate and inspiring people who, from campaigners to coffee farmers, are all experts in what they do. There are opportunities to work in Oxfam's UK headquarters in Oxford, in a regional office, or in one of nearly 700 shops. Interns get to put their skills to great, poverty ending use from day one. Whether that's making Oxfam's High Street presence shine as a voluntary assistant shop manager, or helping to raise vital funds as a marketing and communications assistant. Other possible roles include working in HR and recruitment to support Oxfam's staff around the world, or helping to prepare Oxfam's powerful political campaigns as a research executive.

Joining Oxfam as an intern is a great way to experience how a major international charity operates. Taking on global issues that keep people poor like inequality, discrimination against women and climate change is at the heart of everything they do. In just 15 years extreme poverty has been halved. Apply now and be part of the generation that ends it for good.

STARTING SALARY FOR 2018
£Voluntary

UNIVERSITY VISITS IN 2017-18
OXFORD, OXFORD BROOKES
Please check with your university careers service for full details of local events.

APPLICATION DEADLINE
Year-round recruitment

FURTHER INFORMATION
www.Top100GraduateEmployers.com
Register now for the latest news, campus events, work experience and graduate vacancies at Oxfam.

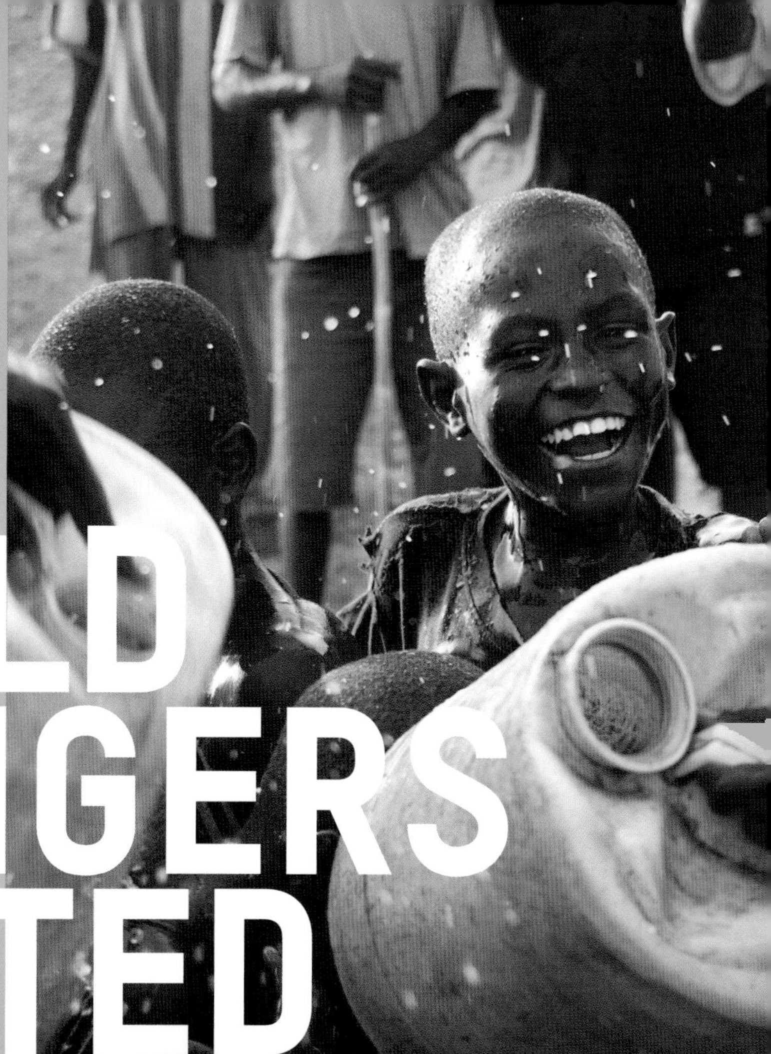

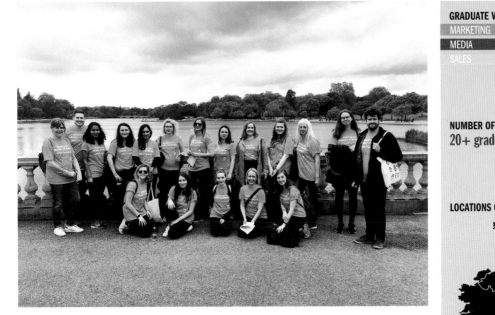

GRADUATE VACANCIES IN 2018

MARKETING

MEDIA

SALES

NUMBER OF VACANCIES

20+ graduate jobs

LOCATIONS OF VACANCIES

Penguin Random House UK connects the world with the stories, ideas and writing that matter. As the biggest publisher in the UK, the diversity of its publishing includes brands such as Jamie Oliver, James Patterson and Peppa Pig through to literary prize winners such as Zadie Smith and Richard Flanagan.

Career opportunities range from the creative teams in Editorial, Marketing, Publicity and Design through to teams in Digital, Finance, Technology, Sales and Publishing Operations to name but a few.

Their flagship entry-level programme, called 'The Scheme', focuses on a different role each year; previous years' intakes have been Marketing, Editorial and Publicity.

They value Purpose, Adventure, Openness, Trust and Heart. Whether someone is motivated by working on something new, or taking the next step in their careers, the business is committed to supporting its colleagues and giving them a workplace that is somewhere they want to be.

The business is comprised of nine publishing houses which each has their own imprints, markets and personality, including a fast-growing Audio publishing division.

They work with a wide range of talent – from storytellers, animators and developers to entrepreneurs, toy manufacturers, producers and, of course, writers. This means that they are similar to broadcasters as they find increasingly more ways to bring stories and ideas to life.

Penguin Random House UK has three publishing sites in London; Vauxhall Bridge Road, Strand and Ealing Broadway; distribution centres in Frating, Grantham and Rugby; and a number of regional offices. They employ over 2,000 people in the UK.

STARTING SALARY FOR 2018

£Competitive

UNIVERSITY VISITS IN 2017-18

Please check with your university careers service for full details of local events.

APPLICATION DEADLINE

Year-round recruitment

Early application advised.

FURTHER INFORMATION

www.Top100GraduateEmployers.com

Register now for the latest news, campus events, work experience and graduate vacancies at Penguin Random House.

Your Story Starts Here

Finding a great story - editor, publisher, sales director, finance team. Making it look good - designer, copy writer, art director, illustrator. Making the finished book - production controller, product manager, quality controller. Getting it out there - marketing assistant, publicity manager, sales executive, social media manager.

Come and be part of the first of a new kind of publisher that captures the attention of the world through the stories, ideas and writing that matter.

Penguin
Random House
UK

POLICE:NOW
INFLUENCE FOR GENERATIONS

www.policenow.org.uk
facebook.com/PoliceNow **f**   graduates@policenow.org.uk ✉
uk.linkedin.com/company/police-now **in**   twitter.com/police_now **y**

GRADUATE VACANCIES IN 2018
POLICING

NUMBER OF VACANCIES
350 graduate jobs

LOCATIONS OF VACANCIES

Police Now's Graduate Leadership Programme offers outstanding graduates the opportunity to pursue a highly ambitious vision for social change. Its aim? To break the intergenerational cycle of crime in the most challenged areas by creating safe, confident communities in which people can thrive.

This two-year programme operates at pace and intensity. And the challenge is unique.

Graduates become fully warranted police officers with responsibility for an area that could be home to as many as 20,000 people. They get to know their communities – the problems, the prominent offenders and the crime hotspots within them. And right from the beginning, they are expected to use innovative ideas and tactics to tackle the toughest problems and deliver high impact results.

The programme is challenging. But graduates are supported by mentors, coaches and line managers. Frontline training is delivered by over 40 different experts and a whole range of operational police officers. And there are opportunities to undertake prestigious secondments with Police Now's partner organisations, which give graduates exposure to the wide range of options available to them once they complete the Police Now programme.

This is a challenge that extends beyond the basic mission of the police to prevent crime and disorder. It's the chance to be a leader in society and on the policing frontline.

And as the 2018 Police Now cohort is expanding to work with over 20 forces across England, it means there are now more opportunities for outstanding graduates to step forward and change the story, not just today but for generations to come.

STARTING SALARY FOR 2018
£29,607
For London positions –
regional differences apply.

UNIVERSITY VISITS IN 2017-18
BIRMINGHAM, BRISTOL, CAMBRIDGE, CARDIFF, DURHAM, EXETER, KING'S COLLEGE LONDON, LANCASTER, LEEDS, LEICESTER, LIVERPOOL, MANCHESTER, NOTTINGHAM, OXFORD, SHEFFIELD, SOUTHAMPTON, UNIVERSITY COLLEGE LONDON, YORK
Please check with your university careers
service for full details of local events.

MINIMUM ENTRY REQUIREMENTS
2.1 Degree
Plus a C grade in English at GCSE.

APPLICATION DEADLINE
1st March 2018
For a July start date.

FURTHER INFORMATION
www.Top100GraduateEmployers.com
Register now for the latest news, campus
events, work experience and graduate
*vacancies at **Police Now**.*

Nearly one in three people aged 65+ worry about being affected by crime.

Join us.
Change the story.

National Graduate Leadership Programme

Their mums were scared to leave the house at night too. Nothing's changed. The same tough neighbourhoods, the same threatening people, the same bad feelings. This is the world as it stands. But there are ways out.

Police Now is a **two-year programme** that offers the top graduates the opportunity to become Police Officers and transform communities. Not just for people today but for generations to come.

The challenge is unique. The environment is high paced. And you can lead the change here **policenow.org.uk**

POLICE:NOW
INFLUENCE FOR GENERATIONS

pwc

The opportunity of a lifetime

pwc

Opportunities are at the heart of a career with PwC. Their purpose is to build trust in society, solving important problems for their clients; helping them tackle business challenges, improving how they work. Graduates can join Assurance, Actuarial, Consulting, Deals, Legal, Tax or Technology.

PwC's continued success, size and scale, not forgetting their extensive client base, creates an environment where undergraduates and graduates get access to the best career and work experience opportunities. They choose the best people to join them, but it might be surprising to learn they're from a wide range of backgrounds and have studied all sorts of degree subjects. With offices UK-wide, PwC are looking for graduates eager to learn, with business awareness, intellectual and cultural curiosity and the ability to build strong relationships. PwC's purpose is to identify and resolve their clients' most pressing issues, and they provide graduates with an opportunity to make a positive impact on society.

Graduates get access to the best learning and development around; learning by doing, learning from others and through formal training. For some business areas this could mean the opportunity to work towards a professional qualification. With PwC, graduates are in the driving seat of their career and supported by a structured development programme.

For undergraduates and graduates exploring work experience opportunities, or ways to help them decide where their skills, interests and career goals could best fit, they could attend a PwC career open day, or apply to a summer internship or work placement. Join PwC. They're focused on helping graduates reach their full potential while providing a competitive salary and a personally tailored benefits package. Take the opportunity of a lifetime.

GRADUATE VACANCIES IN 2018

ACCOUNTANCY

CONSULTING

FINANCE

IT

LAW

NUMBER OF VACANCIES
1,200 graduate jobs

LOCATIONS OF VACANCIES

Vacancies also available in Europe, Asia, the USA and elsewhere in the world.

STARTING SALARY FOR 2018
£Competitive
Plus holiday entitlement, a bike scheme, discounted gym membership and healthcare.

UNIVERSITY VISITS IN 2017-18
ABERDEEN, ASTON, BATH, BELFAST, BIRMINGHAM, BRISTOL, CAMBRIDGE, CARDIFF, DUNDEE, DURHAM, EAST ANGLIA, EDINBURGH, EXETER, GLASGOW, HERIOT-WATT, HULL, IMPERIAL COLLEGE LONDON, LEEDS, LEICESTER, LIVERPOOL, LONDON SCHOOL OF ECONOMICS, LOUGHBOROUGH, MANCHESTER, NEWCASTLE, NOTTINGHAM, NOTTINGHAM TRENT, OXFORD, PLYMOUTH, READING, SHEFFIELD, SOUTHAMPTON, ST ANDREWS, STRATHCLYDE, SURREY, SWANSEA, ULSTER, UNIVERSITY COLLEGE LONDON, WARWICK, YORK
Please check with your university careers service for full details of local events.

MINIMUM ENTRY REQUIREMENTS
2.1 Degree

APPLICATION DEADLINE
Varies by function

FURTHER INFORMATION
www.Top100GraduateEmployers.com
Register now for the latest news, campus events, work experience and graduate vacancies at PwC.

Our training & development is designed to help you excel in your career

Economics degree

Your degree is just the start

Arts degree

Science degree

History degree

50% of our graduate intake studied non-business related subjects

Geography degree

pwc.com/uk/careers

ROYAL AIR FORCE
REGULAR & RESERVE

GRADUATE VACANCIES IN 2018

- ACCOUNTANCY
- ENGINEERING
- FINANCE
- GENERAL MANAGEMENT
- HUMAN RESOURCES
- IT
- LAW
- LOGISTICS
- RESEARCH & DEVELOPMENT
- SALES

NUMBER OF VACANCIES
500-600 graduate jobs

LOCATIONS OF VACANCIES

With cutting edge technology, hundreds of aircraft and more than 30,000 active personnel, the Royal Air Force (RAF) is a key part of the British Armed Forces, defending the UK and its interests, strengthening international peace and stability, as well as being a force for good in the world.

Its people lie at the heart of the RAF; they're looking for professionalism, dedication and courage to achieve the RAF's vision of being 'an agile, adaptable and capable Air Force that, person for person, is second to none, and that makes a decisive air power contribution in support of the UK Defence Mission'.

The world is a changing place and so is the Royal Air Force; it is becoming a smaller, more dynamic force able to carry out its missions. To meet the changing times and challenges, and because of the greater capability of technology, the number of people in the RAF has reduced in recent years. Recruiting people of the right quality is therefore a key part of the RAF's vision for the future.

The RAF encompasses all aspects of operations, including the use of the very latest hi-tech equipment but the centre of the RAF's vision has always been its people – and it always will be. It prides itself on attracting the highest quality recruits from all sectors of society and provides first-class training and continuing development.

Officers in the Royal Air Force are expected to lead from the front, setting standards for the men and women under their command. For graduates, there are more than twenty different career opportunities, including Aircrew, Logistics, Engineering and Personnel roles, as well as medical opportunities for qualified doctors, nurses and dentists. In return the RAF offers a competitive salary, free medical & dental, travel opportunities and world class training. It's no ordinary job.

STARTING SALARY FOR 2018
£30,000+

UNIVERSITY VISITS IN 2017-18
ABERDEEN, BATH, BELFAST, BIRMINGHAM, BRADFORD, BRISTOL, BRUNEL, CAMBRIDGE, CARDIFF, CITY, DUNDEE, DURHAM, EAST ANGLIA, EDINBURGH, ESSEX, EXETER, GLASGOW, HULL, KENT, LANCASTER, LEEDS, LEICESTER, LIVERPOOL, LOUGHBOROUGH, MANCHESTER, NEWCASTLE, NORTHUMBRIA, NOTTINGHAM, NOTTINGHAM TRENT, OXFORD, PLYMOUTH, READING, SHEFFIELD, SOUTHAMPTON, ST ANDREWS, STIRLING, STRATHCLYDE, SURREY, SUSSEX, SWANSEA, ULSTER, YORK
Please check with your university careers service for full details of local events.

MINIMUM ENTRY REQUIREMENTS
Relevant degree required for some roles.

APPLICATION DEADLINE
Year-round recruitment
Early application advised.

FURTHER INFORMATION
www.Top100GraduateEmployers.com
*Register now for the latest news, campus events, work experience and graduate vacancies at the **Royal Air Force**.*

ROYAL AIR FORCE
REGULAR & RESERVE

"So you think you've got what it takes to be an officer in the RAF"

There are graduate careers and then there are graduate challenges - we'd like to think we're the latter. Our officers don't just have good promotion prospects, they get competitive pay and world-class training, as well as six weeks' paid holiday a year, subsidised food and accommodation, free healthcare, and free access to our sports facilities.

As well as specialist training, you'll learn valuable leadership and management skills; you'll also have the opportunity to take part in adventurous training such as rock climbing, skiing and sailing. As you develop your career, you'll move on to face new challenges and opportunities for promotion - both in the UK and overseas.

Interested? If you think you've got what it takes to be an Officer in the RAF, take a look at the RAF Recruitment website at the roles available, what's required for entry and the 24 week Initial Officer Training Course at RAF College Cranwell. You could also be eligible for sponsorship through your sixth-form or university courses, depending on the role you're interested in. We're currently recruiting Engineers, but have opportunities in Logistics, Medical, Personnel, Intelligence and Aircrew Officer roles. Visit the Education and Funding page of the website to find out about the opportunities available.

Healthcare in action

If you've just completed a relevant medical degree, the RAF can offer you a career filled with variety and adventure, as well as first-class postgraduate and specialist training. Once you've been accepted you'll spend 13 weeks at RAF College Cranwell doing the Specialist Entrants Officer Training Course.

www.raf.mod.uk/recruitment/lifestyle-benefits/education-funding/

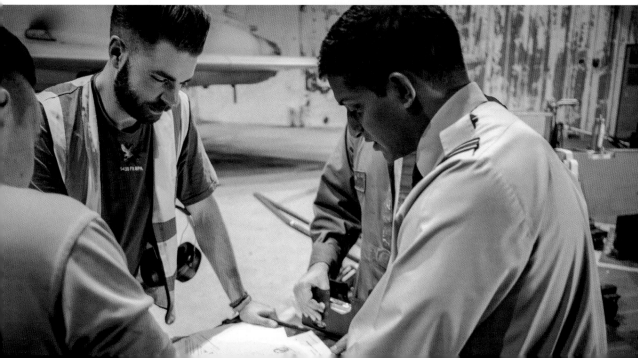

ROYAL NAVY

Throughout the course of history, a life at sea has always attracted those with a taste for travel and adventure; but there are plenty of other reasons for graduates and final-year students to consider a challenging and wide-ranging career with the Royal Navy.

The Royal Navy is, first and foremost, a fighting force. Serving alongside Britain's allies in conflicts around the world, it also vitally protects UK ports, fishing grounds and merchant ships, helping to combat international smuggling, terrorism and piracy. Increasingly, its 30,000 personnel are involved in humanitarian and relief missions; situations where their skills, discipline and resourcefulness make a real difference to people's lives.

Graduates are able to join the Royal Navy as Officers – the senior leadership and management team in the various branches, which range from Engineering, Air and Warfare to Medical, the Fleet Air Arm and Logistics. Starting salaries of at least £25,984 – rising to £31,232 in the first year – compare well with those in industry.

Those wanting to join the Royal Navy as an Engineer – with Marine, Weapon or Air Engineer Officer, above or below the water – could work on anything from sensitive electronics to massive gas-turbine engines and nuclear weapons. What's more, the Royal Navy can offer a secure, flexible career and the potential to extend to age 50.

The Royal Navy offers opportunities for early responsibility, career development, sport, recreation and travel which exceed any in civilian life. With its global reach and responsibilities, the Royal Navy still offers plenty of adventure and the chance to see the world, while pursuing one of the most challenging, varied and fulfilling careers available.

ROYAL NAVY

YOU MAKE A DIFFERENCE NOT MAKE UP THE NUMBERS

ROYAL NAVY OFFICER

Being an officer in the Royal Navy is a career like any other, but the circumstances and places are sometimes extraordinary. With opportunities ranging from Engineer Officer to Medical Officer, it's a responsible, challenging career that will take you further than you've been before. If you want more than just a job, join the Royal Navy and live a life without limits.

LIFE WITHOUT LIMITS
08456 07 55 55
ROYALNAVY.MOD.UK/CAREERS

Santander is one of the largest and most successful financial groups in the world, and their ambition is to become the best bank for their customers, investors and employees. With an eye on the future, they recognise that technology is rapidly changing how customers bank and pay on the move and they are working to be at the forefront of that change.

Motivated by strong team work, an innovative approach to technology, market-leading incentive packages, and a culture of support, they deliver their personal best, every day. Santander focuses on giving graduates everything they need to thrive as future leaders in their chosen areas. That means if they're genuinely passionate, and bring an enthusiasm to their role, graduates are in a great position to develop the skills, experiences and relationships that will kick-start their careers.

Graduate schemes within the business are split into the following divisions – Retail and Business Banking, Global and Corporate Banking further complemented by specialist, operational and support functions. Each is designed to give an in-depth understanding of what makes Santander tick. That could mean developing innovative products for their customers, identifying ways to improve processes for colleagues, or building relationships with high-profile clients.

Whatever the area, graduates will be making a difference from the start. This includes a Corporate Social Responsibility event for Santander's charity of the year – where the aim is to support one million people in their communities by 2020.

What's more, graduates will be part of a structured training scheme which is split into four learning cycles and ends with an industry-recognised qualification (CIOBS) in their chosen area. Add this to a dedicated graduate manager for each programme during the entire scheme, as well as continuous development – there are plenty of benefits and no shortage of opportunities to grow with Santander.

GRADUATE VACANCIES IN 2018
FINANCE
GENERAL MANAGEMENT
RETAILING

NUMBER OF VACANCIES
Up to 50 graduate jobs

LOCATIONS OF VACANCIES

STARTING SALARY FOR 2018
£30,000

UNIVERSITY VISITS IN 2017-18
BIRMINGHAM, BRISTOL, IMPERIAL COLLEGE LONDON, LEICESTER, LONDON SCHOOL OF ECONOMICS, LOUGHBOROUGH, NOTTINGHAM, QUEEN MARY LONDON, SHEFFIELD, UNIVERSITY COLLEGE LONDON, WARWICK, YORK
Please check with your university careers service for full details of local events.

MINIMUM ENTRY REQUIREMENTS
2.1 Degree
280 UCAS points

APPLICATION DEADLINE
February 2018

FURTHER INFORMATION
www.Top100GraduateEmployers.com
Register now for the latest news, campus events, work experience and graduate vacancies at Santander.

You want a better future
We'll help you realise it

Our Emerging Talent programmes provide everything you'll need to realise your future. We'll help you build the relationships that will influence your entire career, and with a combination of dedicated online and in-person teaching as well as on-the job training you'll learn from some of the most talented colleagues in the business. So, if you're passionate about making our banking products and services simple, personal and fair, we have a programme for you.

Realise your future, apply today: www.santanderjobs.co.uk/realiseyourfuture

savills.co.uk/graduates

facebook.com/Savills **f**   gradrecruitment@savills.com ✉

instagram.com/savills_instagrad ⃝   twitter.com/savillsgraduate ✆

savills

GRADUATE VACANCIES IN 2018

PROPERTY

NUMBER OF VACANCIES

90 graduate jobs

LOCATIONS OF VACANCIES

STARTING SALARY FOR 2018

£26,000

£23,000 in the regions.
Plus a £1,000 sign-on bonus.

UNIVERSITY VISITS IN 2017-18
ABERDEEN, BATH, BIRMINGHAM, BRISTOL,
CAMBRIDGE, CARDIFF, CITY, DURHAM,
EDINBURGH, EXETER, GLASGOW,
LEEDS, MANCHESTER, NORTHUMBRIA,
NOTTINGHAM TRENT, OXFORD BROOKES,
PLYMOUTH, READING, SHEFFIELD,
SOUTHAMPTON, UNIVERSITY
COLLEGE LONDON
Please check with your university careers
service for full details of local events.

APPLICATION DEADLINE

Varies by function

FURTHER INFORMATION
www.Top100GraduateEmployers.com
Register now for the latest news, campus
events, work experience and graduate
vacancies at Savills.

Savills UK is a leading global real estate service provider listed on the London Stock Exchange. The company employs over 30,000 staff and has 700 offices and associates worldwide, providing all trainees with excellent scope for international experience as their careers develop.

Savills passionately believe their graduates are future leaders and as such make a huge investment in them. Savills graduates are given responsibility from day one, in teams who highly value their contribution, allowing them to be involved in some of the world's most high-profile property deals and developments. Graduates are surrounded by expert professionals and experienced team members from whom they learn and seek advice. Individual achievement is rewarded and Savills look for bold graduates with entrepreneurial flair.

Savills are proud to be The Times Graduate Employer of Choice for Property for the eleventh year running. Great work life balance, structured training and a dynamic working environment are amongst the factors which see Savills nominated by final year students as the preferred Property employer year on year.

Savills's Graduate Programme offers the chance to gain an internationally recognised Professional qualification. There are roles within Surveying, Planning and Food & Farming, with half of Savills Graduate Programme vacancies positioned outside of London. The company has offices in exciting locations around the UK where Fee Earners work with high-profile and important clients. The diversity of Savills services means there is the flexibility to carve out a fulfilling, individual and self-tailored career path regardless of the location.

SHAPE **Y**OUR FUTURE

40% of our board joined us as graduates

Do you have what it takes?

Become the future of Savills

GRADUATE VACANCIES IN 2018

ENGINEERING

FINANCE

GENERAL MANAGEMENT

HUMAN RESOURCES

IT

LOGISTICS

MARKETING

PURCHASING

RESEARCH & DEVELOPMENT

NUMBER OF VACANCIES
60+ graduate jobs

LOCATIONS OF VACANCIES

STARTING SALARY FOR 2018
£33,000
Plus competitive bonus.

UNIVERSITY VISITS IN 2017-18
ABERDEEN, CAMBRIDGE, HERIOT-WATT,
IMPERIAL COLLEGE LONDON, LEEDS,
LONDON SCHOOL OF ECONOMICS,
MANCHESTER, OXFORD, STRATHCLYDE,
UNIVERSITY COLLEGE LONDON
*Please check with your university careers
service for full details of local events.*

MINIMUM ENTRY REQUIREMENTS
Relevant degree required for some roles.

APPLICATION DEADLINE
Varies by function

FURTHER INFORMATION
www.Top100GraduateEmployers.com
*Register now for the latest news, campus
events, work experience and graduate
vacancies at Shell.*

Shell is a global group of energy and petrochemicals companies. With approximately 90,000 employees in over 70 countries, its aim is to help meet the world's growing demand for energy in economically, environmentally and socially responsible ways.

Shell offers a wide range of career routes. The scale and global reach of the business means they have a huge range of technical, commercial and corporate roles.

The Shell Graduate Programme is open to graduates and early career professionals. The Programme focuses on leadership development and prepares graduates to tackle the world's growing energy demand. As society moves towards a low carbon energy system, the company and its people will strive towards a cleaner energy future.

The structured Graduate Programme gives graduates immediate immersion in their business with real, high levels of responsibility from day one. The Programme is typically three years, although this can depend on the area of the business, and graduates usually complete at least two assignments within this time. Throughout, they receive comprehensive support from mentors, work buddies, the graduate network (Energie) and access to senior business leaders.

Shell Assessed Internships are open to penultimate year students. They are usually 12-week placements undertaken over the summer. During this time students are supported through delivery of a live project for which they have responsibility. Project topics are determined based on the student's interests and the needs of the business. Shell Internships are very sought-after roles that give a fantastic insight into a fascinating business – one that has an impact on everyone.

TECHNOLOGY OR CONSULTANCY
WHY NOT CHOOSE BOTH?

DISCOVER THE WORLD
OF OPPORTUNITIES

**Discover your opportunities at
shell.co.uk/graduates**

A global technology and engineering powerhouse, Siemens has been an innovative force throughout every major industrial revolution – from the age of steam power to advances in electrification and then automation. Now this giant of engineering and international business practices is entering phase four of the revolution – digitalisation.

As a world-class authority on manufacturing, power generation, building technologies and the infrastructure making up the modern world, Siemens is propelling the UK ahead in this new era, labelled 'Industry 4.0'.

The Chief Executive of Siemens UK, Juergen Maier, believes they have a responsibility to champion projects which make the world a better place. Pioneering new technologies creates jobs and improves quality of life. The push towards sustainability is also key, and Siemens leads the way when increasing performance and efficiency, simultaneously. They're already developing futuristic technologies such as AI, robotics, driverless cars and MindSphere – a powerful insight into how future cities will connect to the Internet of Things.

Siemens seeks forward-thinking graduates who can launch them to the forefront of just about everything. They have locations across the country, employing the brightest engineers and business minds. New starters can expect to be on the ground, participating in meaningful projects that optimise cutting-edge resources and insights. The culture revolves around ingenuity and inclusion, as well as down-to-earth interaction, preventing hierarchy from obstructing invention. Roles include electrical and mechanical engineering, through to project management and finance. Everyone benefits from a structured two-year Graduate Development Programme, facilitating the essential skills required to succeed in a career at Siemens. This means growing in an environment that's well-known for delivering the very best.

GRADUATE VACANCIES IN 2018

ENGINEERING
FINANCE
GENERAL MANAGEMENT
IT
PURCHASING
RESEARCH & DEVELOPMENT
SALES

NUMBER OF VACANCIES
70-80 graduate jobs

LOCATIONS OF VACANCIES

STARTING SALARY FOR 2018
£Competitive

UNIVERSITY VISITS IN 2017-18
BIRMINGHAM, CAMBRIDGE, IMPERIAL COLLEGE LONDON, LOUGHBOROUGH, MANCHESTER, NEWCASTLE, NOTTINGHAM, OXFORD, SHEFFIELD, SOUTHAMPTON, STRATHCLYDE
Please check with your university careers service for full details of local events.

MINIMUM ENTRY REQUIREMENTS
2.2 Degree

APPLICATION DEADLINE
Early January 2018

FURTHER INFORMATION
www.Top100GraduateEmployers.com
Register now for the latest news, campus events, work experience and graduate vacancies at Siemens.

Brave enough to re-imagine the world around you?

Here at Siemens, we're changing the way the world works. Take MindSphere, our ground-breaking open source operating system for the Internet of Things. It helps businesses develop smart new applications, services and business models – while letting our people push their limits and learn new things every day. Find out more about our graduate programmes and where you fit in by heading to our careers site.

Visit
siemens.co.uk/careers

28 years of experience. 22 million customers. Five countries. Sky, Europe's leading entertainment and communications business, is more than just television, mobile and broadband. With pioneering technology, innovative minds and forward-thinking teams, it makes the future happen.

People drive Sky's success. But the company doesn't look for a certain 'type' of person. And it definitely doesn't look for a certain type of graduate. Instead, with programmes across Software Engineering and Technology, or Commercial programmes in areas like Finance or Marketing, Sky looks out for a whole host of different skills. What graduates do need to succeed, however, is the drive, passion and ambition to write their own career story – whatever their speciality or degree discipline.

Whether applicants want to develop into business leaders, create cutting-edge products and services or specialise in an area of their choice, Sky have a programme to fit. For those students who haven't decided on their career route, Sky also offers insight days, work experience programmes and summer and university placements – giving students the chance to begin their career story.

Sky believes in better. Better roles. Better opportunities. Better work. For students based at Sky's state-of-the-art offices in London, Leeds or Edinburgh, that means high levels of responsibility – allowing them to see the impact of their work. And with hands-on training and on-the-job learning, bright new talent can learn everything it takes to keep audiences entertained. Whatever their skills, wherever they join, from day one graduates will be part of a friendly network that stretches right across the business. Add to that flexible working, structured learning plans, competitive rewards and discounts, and students have everything they need to flourish.

GRADUATE VACANCIES IN 2018

FINANCE
IT
MARKETING

NUMBER OF VACANCIES
90+ graduate jobs

LOCATIONS OF VACANCIES

STARTING SALARY FOR 2018
£25,000-£32,000

UNIVERSITY VISITS IN 2017-18
BATH, BRISTOL, BRUNEL, CITY, DURHAM, EDINBURGH, GLASGOW, HERIOT-WATT, IMPERIAL COLLEGE LONDON, KENT, LEEDS, LIVERPOOL, LONDON SCHOOL OF ECONOMICS, LOUGHBOROUGH, MANCHESTER, NEWCASTLE, NOTTINGHAM, READING, ROYAL HOLLOWAY, SHEFFIELD, SOUTHAMPTON, STRATHCLYDE, SURREY, UNIVERSITY COLLEGE LONDON, WARWICK, YORK
Please check with your university careers service for full details of local events.

APPLICATION DEADLINE
Varies by function

FURTHER INFORMATION
www.Top100GraduateEmployers.com
Register now for the latest news, campus events, work experience and graduate vacancies at Sky.

Introducing

The future stars

Tamera
"The coding guru"

Tristan
"The programming pro"

Phoebe
"The visionary"

Dhiren
"The innovator"

Daisy
"The analytical one"

Sky Early Careers

Doers. Thinkers. Fixers. Innovators. Challengers. All sorts of bright new talent are writing their own stories at Sky – the heart of entertainment and technology. And, with world-class support, a range of graduate, placement, and work experience programmes plus proper responsibility from the start, you could be one of them. So what are you waiting for? Start your story today.

Search 'Sky Early Careers' to find out more.

sky

SLAUGHTER AND MAY

www.slaughterandmay.com
trainee.recruit@slaughterandmay.com

Slaughter and May is one of the most prestigious law firms in the world. They advise on high-profile and often landmark international transactions. Their excellent and varied client list ranges from governments to entrepreneurs, from retailers to entertainment companies and from conglomerates to Premier League football clubs.

Slaughter and May has offices in London, Brussels, Hong Kong and Beijing and close relationships with leading independent law firms around the world.

Slaughter and May has built a reputation for delivering innovative solutions to difficult problems. This reputation has been earned because each of their multi-specialist lawyers advises on broad legal areas, combining experience gained on one type of transaction to solve problems in another. They are a full service law firm to corporate clients and have leading practitioners across a wide range of practice areas including Mergers and Acquisitions, Corporate and Commercial, Financing, Tax, Competition, Dispute Resolution, Real Estate, Pensions and Employment, Financial Regulation, Information Technology and Intellectual Property.

Their lawyers are not set billing or time targets and are therefore free to concentrate on what matters most – expertise, sound judgement, a willingness to help one another and the highest quality of client service.

During the two-year training contract, trainees turn their hand to a broad range of work, taking an active role in four, five or six groups while sharing an office with a partner or experienced associate. All trainees spend at least two six-month seats in the firm's market leading corporate, commercial and financing groups. Subject to gaining some contentious experience, they choose how to spend the remaining time.

Among their lawyers, 38 nationalities and 83 different universities are represented.

GRADUATE VACANCIES IN 2018
LAW

NUMBER OF VACANCIES
80-85 graduate jobs
For training contracts starting in 2020.

LOCATIONS OF VACANCIES

STARTING SALARY FOR 2018
£43,000

UNIVERSITY VISITS IN 2017-18
ABERDEEN, BIRMINGHAM, BRISTOL, CAMBRIDGE, DURHAM, EDINBURGH, EXETER, GLASGOW, KING'S COLLEGE LONDON, LANCASTER, LEEDS, LONDON SCHOOL OF ECONOMICS, MANCHESTER, NEWCASTLE, NOTTINGHAM, OXFORD, QUEEN MARY LONDON, SHEFFIELD, ST ANDREWS, UNIVERSITY COLLEGE DUBLIN, UNIVERSITY COLLEGE LONDON, WARWICK, YORK
Please check with your university careers service for full details of local events.

MINIMUM ENTRY REQUIREMENTS
2.1 Degree

APPLICATION DEADLINE
Please see website for full details.

FURTHER INFORMATION
www.Top100GraduateEmployers.com
*Register now for the latest news, campus events, work experience and graduate vacancies at **Slaughter and May**.*

SLAUGHTER AND MAY

A world of difference

Laws, international markets, global institutions… all changing every day. So how do we, as an international law firm, create the agility of mind that enables us to guide some of the world's most influential organisations into the future?

By allowing bright people the freedom to grow. By training lawyers in a way that develops a closer understanding of clients through working on a wider range of transactions. By fostering an ethos of knowledge sharing, support and mutual development by promoting from within and leaving the clocks outside when it comes to billing. To learn more about how our key differences not only make a world of difference to our clients, but also to our lawyers and their careers, visit

slaughterandmay.com/careers

80
training contracts

250+
workshops
and schemes

Lawyers from
83
universities

TeachFirst

teachfirst.org.uk/graduates

facebook.com/TeachFirst **f** faq@teachfirst.org.uk ✉

linkedin.com/company/Teach-First **in** twitter.com/TeachFirst **y**

instagram.com/teachfirstuk **◯** youtube.com/TeachFirstUK ▶

STAND UP FOR GENIUS.
IT EXISTS IN ALL OF US.

How much a person achieves in life should not be determined by how much their parents earn. Yet in the UK, it usually is. Teach First wants to change this by building a movement of leaders who change lives within classrooms, schools and across society.

Since 2002 Teach First has been training and supporting outstanding graduates to do just that. Over 10,000 people have already joined their Leadership Development Programme (LDP) and gone on to become inspirational classroom and school leaders, or energetic advocates for change through their roles in business, the third sector and government.

Teach First describes the LDP as a career-defining opportunity. The two-year paid programme is based on global best practice and research. It comprises world-class teaching and leadership training with a fully-funded Post-Graduate Diploma in Education (PGDE) and leads to Qualified Teacher Status. It includes the option to top up the PGDE to a Master's degree that is specifically designed to further develop participants' effectiveness as leaders and teachers.

Being part of the LDP also gives participants access to some of the most influential organisations and experts in the professional world – a diverse range of connections who share a commitment to ending educational inequality and value the skills and experiences that participants gain through the programme.

Teach First participants come from a multitude of backgrounds and have different plans for the future. But all have one thing in common: They join Teach First to lead a movement that changes lives within classrooms, schools and across society. Apply now for this career-defining opportunity.

GRADUATE VACANCIES IN 2018

TEACHING

NUMBER OF VACANCIES
1,750 graduate jobs

LOCATIONS OF VACANCIES

STARTING SALARY FOR 2018
£Competitive

UNIVERSITY VISITS IN 2017-18
ABERYSTWYTH, ASTON, BANGOR, BATH, BIRMINGHAM, BRISTOL, BRUNEL, CAMBRIDGE, CARDIFF, CITY, DURHAM, EAST ANGLIA, EDINBURGH, ESSEX, EXETER, GLASGOW, HULL, IMPERIAL COLLEGE LONDON, KING'S COLLEGE LONDON, KENT, LANCASTER, LEEDS, LEICESTER, LIVERPOOL, LONDON SCHOOL OF ECONOMICS, LOUGHBOROUGH, MANCHESTER, NEWCASTLE, NORTHUMBRIA, NOTTINGHAM, NOTTINGHAM TRENT, OXFORD, OXFORD BROOKES, QUEEN MARY LONDON, READING, ROYAL HOLLOWAY, SHEFFIELD, SOUTHAMPTON, ST ANDREWS, SURREY, SUSSEX, SWANSEA, ULSTER, UNIVERSITY COLLEGE LONDON, WARWICK, YORK
Please check with your university careers service for full details of local events.

MINIMUM ENTRY REQUIREMENTS
2.1 Degree

APPLICATION DEADLINE
Year-round recruitment
Early application advised.

FURTHER INFORMATION
www.Top100GraduateEmployers.com
Register now for the latest news, campus events, work experience and graduate vacancies at **Teach First***.*

FIND WAYS TO OPEN MINDS, OPEN EYES AND OPEN DOORS.

FIND YOUR WAY TO LEAD.

Give every child the belief that they can achieve anything. Develop skills that could take you anywhere. We find, train and support people to become inspirational leaders in the classroom, in schools and across all sectors of society. Find out more at **teachfirst.org.uk/graduates**

Each child. Each future.

TeachFirst

Teach First is a registered charity (1098294)

TESCO

Tesco is passionate about serving shoppers a little better every day and its colleagues are at the heart of that. Their graduates are incredibly important to them. From day one, Tesco gives graduates real responsibilities and supports them to develop and grow throughout the programme.

A business of Tesco's scale provides a whole host of opportunities – it runs successful store, distribution and office programmes, and will support its graduates to develop the career path that's right for them. No two days are the same at Tesco and this, coupled with its fast-paced and vibrant culture, is something the company is really proud of.

Tesco firmly believes that the most rewarding way for graduates to learn is through the responsibility of real-life business experience, which they get from day one. They can apply their knowledge, by being innovative, working collaboratively across the business, and being responsive to the business' needs.

Tesco lays on masterclasses and leadership development training that's unique to them, in addition to programme-specific learning, to support graduates throughout their journey. Graduates also have access to a mentor and a buddy, who will be there to help as they grow and develop.

The company understands that colleagues should enjoy their work surroundings and outdoor space in order to maximise productivity. Their Welwyn Garden City campus offers just that, with beautifully landscaped outdoor areas and plenty of space for walking meetings, as well as a jungle gym for those wanting to exercise outdoors. There is also a subsidised gym that is free to use during flexible working hours for those who prefer to exercise indoors. And that's not all. Tesco looks forward to opening its very own state-of-the-art learning centre and Tesco Express store in 2018.

GRADUATE VACANCIES IN 2018

ENGINEERING
FINANCE
GENERAL MANAGEMENT
IT
LOGISTICS
MARKETING
PURCHASING
RETAILING

NUMBER OF VACANCIES
100+ graduate jobs

LOCATIONS OF VACANCIES

STARTING SALARY FOR 2018
£26,000-£32,000

UNIVERSITY VISITS IN 2017-18
BIRMINGHAM, BRISTOL, CAMBRIDGE, DURHAM, GLASGOW, IMPERIAL COLLEGE LONDON, KING'S COLLEGE LONDON, KENT, MANCHESTER, NORTHUMBRIA, NOTTINGHAM, SHEFFIELD, WARWICK
Please check with your university careers service for full details of local events.

MINIMUM ENTRY REQUIREMENTS
2.1 Degree

APPLICATION DEADLINE
14th January 2018

FURTHER INFORMATION
www.Top100GraduateEmployers.com
Register now for the latest news, campus events, work experience and graduate vacancies at **Tesco**.

Let's grow together.

We like to help our graduates to grow. That's why we give them responsibility from day one. We also lay on masterclasses and unique leadership development. Plus there's plenty more support on hand, like a mentor, a 'buddy' who's been in your shoes, and the flexibility to develop in a way that works for you.

Find out more at **tesco-careers.com/graduates**

The Think Ahead programme is a new route into social work, for graduates and career-changers remarkable enough to make a real difference to people with mental health problems. The paid, two-year programme combines on-the-job learning, a Masters degree and leadership training.

Mental health social workers use therapy, support, and advocacy to enable people to manage the social factors in their lives – like relationships, housing, and employment – to allow them to get well and stay well.

The Think Ahead programme focusses on adult community mental health teams, supporting people living with a wide variety of illnesses such as bipolar disorder, schizophrenia, and personality disorders. These are multi-disciplinary teams, usually within an NHS Trust, which can include social workers, nurses, support workers, occupational therapists, psychologists and psychiatrists.

Participants on the programme begin their training with an intensive six-week residential over the summer. This prepares them for frontline work by giving them a grounding in approaches to mental health social work.

Following this training, participants work within NHS mental health teams in units of four. Each unit is led by a highly experienced Consultant Social Worker, and participants share responsibility for the care of the individuals they work with. Participants become professionally qualified in the second year of the programme and are then able to work more independently.

Throughout the programme there is regular training and time allocated for academic study. The programme culminates in a Masters degree in social work. Leadership training also takes place throughout the programme, supporting participants to become excellent social workers, and to work towards leading change in the future.

GRADUATE VACANCIES IN 2018
SOCIAL WORK

NUMBER OF VACANCIES
100 graduate jobs

LOCATIONS OF VACANCIES

STARTING SALARY FOR 2018
£16,900-£18,800+
This is a tax free bursary.

UNIVERSITY VISITS IN 2017-18
ASTON, BATH, BIRMINGHAM, BRISTOL, CAMBRIDGE, CARDIFF, CITY, EAST ANGLIA, EDINBURGH, EXETER, IMPERIAL COLLEGE LONDON, KING'S COLLEGE LONDON, LEEDS, LIVERPOOL, LONDON SCHOOL OF ECONOMICS, LOUGHBOROUGH, MANCHESTER, NEWCASTLE, NOTTINGHAM, OXFORD, QUEEN MARY LONDON, SCHOOL OF AFRICAN STUDIES, SHEFFIELD, SOUTHAMPTON, SUSSEX, UNIVERSITY COLLEGE LONDON, WARWICK, YORK
Please check with your university careers service for full details of local events.

MINIMUM ENTRY REQUIREMENTS
2.1 Degree

APPLICATION DEADLINE
December 2017
Early application advised.

FURTHER INFORMATION
www.Top100GraduateEmployers.com
*Register now for the latest news, campus events, work experience and graduate vacancies at **Think Ahead**.*

THINK
AHEAD

"

I'm driven by helping people with mental health problems to enjoy their lives and take steps towards getting well.

Nottingham graduate and
Think Ahead participant

thinkahead.org

www.unilever.co.uk/careers/graduates/uflp

enquiry@unilevergraduates.com ✉

twitter.com/UnileverGradsUK 🐦 facebook.com/UnileverCareersUKandIRE f

www.youtube.com/TheUnileverUFLP ▶ linkedin.com/company/Unilever in

@unilevergradsUK 👻 instagram.com/unilevergradsuk 📷

Unilever, a leading consumer goods company, makes some of the world's best-loved brands: Dove, Knorr, Magnum, Lynx, Sure, Tresemmé and Hellmann's to name a few. Over two billion consumers use their products every day. Unilever products are sold in 190 countries and they employ 168,000 people globally.

Around the world, Unilever products help people look good, feel good and get more out of life. It's one of the world's greatest businesses, with amazing brands, dynamic people and a sustainable vision. What's Unilever's challenge? To double the size of its business, while reducing its environmental impact and increasing its social impact. Unilever is looking for talented graduates who have the will and the drive to help Unilever achieve this ambition.

Graduates can apply to one of the following areas – Supply Chain Management, Customer Management (Sales), HR Management, Marketing, Technology Management, Research & Development, Research & Development Packaging and Financial Management. The UFLP is about making a big impact on business. It is about growing iconic, market-leading brands from the first day and tapping into continuous business mentoring, excellent training, and hands-on responsibility. Whichever area they join, graduates will have the opportunity to make a positive difference.

Graduates will have real responsibility from day one, an opportunity of becoming a manager after three years, and a great support network to see them develop and attain their future goals. Unilever will support them in achieving Chartered status and qualifications such as CIMA, IMechE, IChemE, IEE, APICS, ICS and CIPD.

With such a great ambition lie exciting challenges for the company and its brands, and a fantastic opportunity for graduates to have a great head start in their career, make a real difference to Unilever's business and the world!

GRADUATE VACANCIES IN 2018

ENGINEERING
FINANCE
HUMAN RESOURCES
IT
LOGISTICS
MARKETING
RESEARCH & DEVELOPMENT
SALES

NUMBER OF VACANCIES
45-50 graduate jobs

LOCATIONS OF VACANCIES

Vacancies also available in Europe.

STARTING SALARY FOR 2018
£30,000
Plus benefits and bonus opportunities.

UNIVERSITY VISITS IN 2017-18
ASTON, BATH, BIRMINGHAM, CAMBRIDGE, DURHAM, EXETER, IMPERIAL COLLEGE LONDON, KING'S COLLEGE LONDON, LANCASTER, LEEDS, LIVERPOOL, LOUGHBOROUGH, MANCHESTER, NEWCASTLE, OXFORD, STRATHCLYDE, UNIVERSITY COLLEGE LONDON, WARWICK
Please check with your university careers service for full details of local events.

MINIMUM ENTRY REQUIREMENTS
2.1 Degree

APPLICATION DEADLINE
Year-round Recruitment
Early application advised.

FURTHER INFORMATION
www.Top100GraduateEmployers.com
Register now for the latest news, campus events, work experience and graduate vacancies at Unilever.

GRADUATE VACANCIES IN 2018

FINANCE

GENERAL MANAGEMENT

HUMAN RESOURCES

MARKETING

SALES

NUMBER OF VACANCIES
40+ graduate jobs

LOCATIONS OF VACANCIES

Virgin Media is part of Liberty Global plc, the world's largest international cable company. Serving 5.8 million cable customers and 3 million mobile subscribers across the UK and Ireland, Virgin Media helps to connect people and enable them to experience the endless possibilities of the digital world.

Virgin Media is powering a digital world that makes good things happen. Since the invention of the internet, digital technology has had an increasing impact on the way people live and communicate. But it's not just technology that interests Virgin Media, it's how technology can be used to improve lives and prospects.

Across the UK and Ireland, Virgin Media offers four multi-award winning services – broadband, TV, landline and mobile – and is in the process of growing all aspects of the business so it can connect more of its customers to the things and people they care about.

Virgin Media is looking for the future leaders and experts who can help them stay ahead of the game. In return, its graduates will be put right at the heart of the business – dialling up their strengths, stretching and challenging the norm and broadening their knowledge of the company and the telecoms industry.

Whether a candidate sees their future in finance, marketing or another exciting area of Virgin Media, every graduate will gain the relevant knowledge, skills and experience they need to supercharge a successful career. Virgin Media believes that anything is possible and encourages its graduates to grab new opportunities, get involved and gain invaluable experience through exposure and education.

So, why not join Virgin Media – one of the world's most exciting companies – kick start your career, and make good things happen.

STARTING SALARY FOR 2018
£29,000
Plus a £2,000 welcome bonus, a performance-related bonus and other benefits

UNIVERSITY VISITS IN 2017-18
BATH, BIRMINGHAM, LEEDS, LOUGHBOROUGH, MANCHESTER, READING
Please check with your university careers service for full details of local events.

MINIMUM ENTRY REQUIREMENTS
2.1 Degree
Relevant degree required for some roles.

APPLICATION DEADLINE
Varies by function

FURTHER INFORMATION
www.Top100GraduateEmployers.com
Register now for the latest news, campus events, work experience and graduate vacancies at Virgin Media.

Get on the
ultrafast track

Our growing ultrafast fibre network is powering the UK and Ireland's digital future.
But it's people who really add the magic to our cables.

Bag a spot on Virgin Media's Graduate programme, and you won't just join a Top
Graduate Employer. You'll help us connect more people to everyone and everything
they love — and get your career off to a blisteringly fast start.

Apply today at **virginmediagraduates.co.uk**

wellcome

GRADUATE VACANCIES IN 2018
FINANCE
GENERAL MANAGEMENT
HUMAN RESOURCES
INVESTMENT BANKING
IT
MARKETING
MEDIA
RESEARCH & DEVELOPMENT

NUMBER OF VACANCIES
10-12 graduate jobs

LOCATIONS OF VACANCIES

STARTING SALARY FOR 2018
£26,000+

UNIVERSITY VISITS IN 2017-18
BATH, BIRMINGHAM, BRISTOL, BRUNEL,
CAMBRIDGE, EAST ANGLIA, EDINBURGH,
EXETER, IMPERIAL COLLEGE LONDON,
KING'S COLLEGE LONDON, LEEDS,
LEICESTER, LONDON SCHOOL OF
ECONOMICS, NEWCASTLE, NORTHUMBRIA,
OXFORD, QUEEN MARY LONDON, READING,
SCHOOL OF AFRICAN STUDIES, SHEFFIELD,
UNIVERSITY COLLEGE LONDON
*Please check with your university careers
service for full details of local events.*

MINIMUM ENTRY REQUIREMENTS
2.2 Degree

APPLICATION DEADLINE
Varies by function

FURTHER INFORMATION
www.Top100GraduateEmployers.com
*Register now for the latest news, campus
events, work experience and graduate
vacancies at* **Wellcome.**

Wellcome exists to improve health for everyone by helping great ideas to thrive. Wellcome is a global charitable foundation, both politically and financially independent. It supports scientists and researchers, takes on big problems, fuels imaginations and sparks debate.

Its £20.9 billion investment portfolio gives it the independence to support such transformative work as the sequencing and understanding of the human genome, research that established front-line drugs for malaria, and Wellcome Collection, Wellcome's free venue that explores medicine, life and art.

For recent graduates that want to make a difference in global health, Wellcome offers a two-year graduate development programme. During the programme graduates try out four different jobs for six months at a time. These could involve helping to develop funding schemes, researching investment opportunities or identifying new ways to engage the public. No matter which rotations graduates choose, they'll be a valued member of the team, with support from mentors, line managers and peers, on-the-job and formal training, and the knowledge that they're contributing to Wellcome's overall purpose.

Wellcome is well known for funding scientific and medical research, but more broadly it's interested in the intersection of health, culture and art, and so is looking for graduates from all backgrounds. As well as recruiting scientists who want to stay close to their subject away from the lab, it's previously recruited an engineering graduate who found a passion for communications and an art history graduate who first discovered Wellcome through Wellcome Collection. Its programme is flexible and actively encourages graduates to act boldly, defy expectations, savour the mix that is so readily available and enjoy the challenge, all while developing skills that will be invaluable in the future.

"Your suggestions for change are truly valued... you have the chance to help shape what Wellcome becomes for decades into the future"

Jack, joined Wellcome in 2016

Credit: Jo Metson Scott

White & Case is a global law firm with nearly 2,000 lawyers worldwide. They've built an enviable network of 41 offices in 29 countries. That investment is the foundation for their client work in 159 countries today. Many White & Case clients are multinational organisations with complex needs that require the involvement of multiple offices.

White & Case trainees will work on fast-paced cutting-edge cross-border projects from the outset of their career. In London, the key areas of work include: banking, financial restructuring and insolvency; capital markets (including regulatory compliance, high yield and securitisation); dispute resolution (including antitrust, commercial litigation, intellectual property, international arbitration, trade, white collar and construction and engineering); energy, infrastructure, project and asset finance (EIPAF); corporate (including M&A, private equity, employment, compensation and benefits, investment funds, real estate and tax).

White & Case is looking to recruit ambitious trainees who have a desire to gain hands-on practical experience from day one and a willingness to take charge of their own career. They value globally-minded citizens of the world who are eager to work across borders and cultures, and who are intrigued by solving problems within multiple legal systems.

The training contract consists of four six-month seats, one of which is guaranteed to be spent in one of White & Case's overseas offices, including Abu Dhabi, Beijing, Dubai, Frankfurt, Hong Kong, Moscow, New York, Paris, Prague, Singapore, Stockholm and Tokyo. The remaining three seats can be spent in any one of the firm's practice groups in London. Receiving a high level of partner and senior associate contact from day one, trainees can be confident that they will receive high-quality, stimulating and rewarding work.

GRADUATE VACANCIES IN 2018
LAW

NUMBER OF VACANCIES
50 graduate jobs
For training contracts starting in 2020.

LOCATIONS OF VACANCIES

STARTING SALARY FOR 2018
£46,000

UNIVERSITY VISITS IN 2017-18
BIRMINGHAM, BRISTOL, CAMBRIDGE, DURHAM, EDINBURGH, EXETER, KING'S COLLEGE LONDON, LEEDS, LONDON SCHOOL OF ECONOMICS, MANCHESTER, NOTTINGHAM, OXFORD, QUEEN MARY LONDON, SCHOOL OF AFRICAN STUDIES, SOUTHAMPTON, ST ANDREWS, TRINITY COLLEGE DUBLIN, UNIVERSITY COLLEGE DUBLIN, UNIVERSITY COLLEGE LONDON, WARWICK, YORK
Please check with your university careers service for full details of local events.

MINIMUM ENTRY REQUIREMENTS
2.1 Degree

APPLICATION DEADLINE
Please see website for full details.

FURTHER INFORMATION
www.Top100GraduateEmployers.com
Register now for the latest news, campus events, work experience and graduate vacancies at White & Case.

Together we
make a mark

The future of law is global. If you'd like to
join a firm that guarantees all trainees an
overseas seat, we'd like to hear from you.
whitecase.com/careers

WHITE & CASE

WPP

www.wpp.com

harriet.miller@wpp.com ✉

twitter.com/WPP 🐦   facebook.com/WPP f

youtube.com/WPP ▶   linkedin.com/company/WPP in

WPP is the world's largest communications services group – including Advertising; Media Investment Management; Data Investment Management; Public Relations & Public Affairs; Branding & Identity; Healthcare Communications; Digital, eCommerce & Shopper Marketing and Specialist Communications.

WPP has more than 160 companies setting industry standards and working with many of the world's leading brands, creating communications ideas that help to build business for their clients. Between them, our companies work with 360 of the Fortune Global 500; all 30 of the Dow Jones 30 and 78 of the NASDAQ 100.

Collectively, over 205,000 people (including associates and investments) work for WPP companies, in over 3,000 offices across 112 countries. WPP Fellowships develop high-calibre management talent with unique experience across a range of marketing disciplines. Over three years, Fellows work in three different WPP operating companies, each representing a different marketing communications discipline and geography. Fellows are likely to work in a client management or planning role, although some work on the creative side of an agency. Each rotation is chosen on the basis of the individual's interests and the Group's needs.

Fellowships will be awarded to applicants who are intellectually curious and motivated by the prospect of delivering high-quality communications services to their clients. WPP wants people who are committed to marketing communications, take a rigorous and creative approach to problem-solving and will function well in a flexible, loosely structured work environment. WPP is offering several three-year Fellowships, with competitive remuneration and excellent long term career prospects with WPP. Many former Fellows now occupy senior management positions in WPP companies.

GRADUATE VACANCIES IN 2018
MARKETING
MEDIA

NUMBER OF VACANCIES
1-10 graduate jobs

LOCATIONS OF VACANCIES

Vacancies also available in Europe, Asia, the USA and elsewhere in the world.

STARTING SALARY FOR 2018
£Competitive

UNIVERSITY VISITS IN 2017-18
BRISTOL, CAMBRIDGE, DURHAM, IMPERIAL COLLEGE LONDON, KING'S COLLEGE LONDON, LONDON SCHOOL OF ECONOMICS, OXFORD, QUEEN MARY LONDON, UNIVERSITY COLLEGE LONDON
Please check with your university careers service for full details of local events.

MINIMUM ENTRY REQUIREMENTS
2.1 Degree

APPLICATION DEADLINE
9th November 2017

FURTHER INFORMATION
www.Top100GraduateEmployers.com
Register now for the latest news, campus events, work experience and graduate vacancies at WPP.

WPP
The Fellowship 2018

Ambidextrous brains required

WPP is the world leader in marketing communications, with more than 160 companies setting industry standards in Advertising; Media Investment Management; Data Investment Management; Public Relations & Public Affairs; Branding & Identity; Healthcare Communications; Digital, eCommerce & Shopper Marketing and Specialist Communications.

We are manufacturers of communications ideas that help to build business for our clients, through creating and developing relationships with the people who buy and use their products and services. We do this through a demanding combination of hard work and flair; logic and intuition; left brain and right brain thinking.

The Fellowship was started, 22 years ago, to create future generations of leaders for our companies. Fellows tend to be intellectually curious people who are motivated by the challenges of marketing communications and by the prospect of working at the confluence of art and business. They spend three years on the Program: in each year they work in a different WPP company, in a different marketing communications discipline and, usually, on a different continent.

Long-term prospects within a WPP company are excellent, with many former Fellows now occupying senior management positions.

Deadline for entry:
9 November 2017

Visit our website and apply online at
www.wpp.com

For further information contact:

Harriet Miller, WPP
T: +44 (0)20 7408 2204
E-mail: harriet.miller@wpp.com

Useful Information

EMPLOYER	GRADUATE RECRUITMENT WEBSITE	EMPLOYER	GRADUATE RECRUITMENT WEBSITE
ACCENTURE	accenture.com/timestop100	IRWIN MITCHELL	www.irwinmitchell.com/graduates
AECOM	www.aecom.com/uk-ireland-graduate-careers	JAGUAR LAND ROVER	www.jaguarlandrovercareers.com
AIRBUS	company.airbus.com/careers	J.P. MORGAN	www.jpmorgan.com/careers
ALDI	www.aldirecruitment.co.uk/graduate	KPMG	www.kpmgcareers.co.uk
ALLEN & OVERY	www.aograduate.com	L'ORÉAL	careers.loreal.com/en/ukgrads
AMAZON	www.amazon.jobs	LIDL	www.lidlgraduatecareers.co.uk
ARMY	www.army.mod.uk/belong/officer	LINKLATERS	careers.linklaters.com
ASTRAZENECA	careers.astrazeneca.com/students	LLOYD'S	www.lloyds.com/graduates
ATKINS	careers.atkinsglobal.com	LLOYDS BANKING GROUP	www.lloydsbankinggrouptalent.com
BAE SYSTEMS	www.baesystems.com/graduates	M&S	www.marksandspencergrads.com
BAKER MCKENZIE	bakermckenzie.com/londongraduates	MARS	mars.co.uk/graduates
BANK OF ENGLAND	www.bankofenglandearlycareers.co.uk	MCDONALD'S	people.mcdonalds.co.uk
BARCLAYS	joinus.barclays.com	MCKINSEY & COMPANY	www.mckinsey.com/careers
BBC	www.bbc.co.uk/careers/trainee-schemes	MI5 – THE SECURITY SERVICE	www.mi5.gov.uk/careers
BLOOMBERG	www.bloomberg.com/careers	MORGAN STANLEY	www.morganstanley.com/campus
BMW GROUP	www.bmwgroup.jobs/uk	MOTT MACDONALD	www.mottmac.com/careers/uk-graduate
BOOTS	www.boots.jobs/graduate-schemes	NESTLÉ	www.nestleacademy.co.uk
BP	www.bp.com/grads/uk	NETWORK RAIL	www.networkrail.co.uk/careers/graduates
BT	www.btplc.com/careercentre/earlycareers	NEWTON EUROPE	newtoneurope.com/spirit
CANCER RESEARCH UK	graduates.cancerresearchuk.org	NGDP FOR LOCAL GOVERNMENT	www.ngdp.org.uk
CENTRICA	www.centrica.com/graduates	NHS	www.nhsgraduates.co.uk
CHARITYWORKS	www.charity-works.co.uk	NORTON ROSE FULBRIGHT	www.nortonrosefulbrightgraduates.com
CIVIL SERVICE FAST STREAM	www.faststream.gov.uk	OXFAM	www.oxfam.org.uk
CMS	www.cms.law	PENGUIN RANDOM HOUSE	www.penguinrandomhousecareers.co.uk
DANONE	www.danonegraduates.co.uk	POLICE NOW	www.policenow.org.uk
DELOITTE	deloitte.co.uk/graduates	PWC	pwc.com/uk/careers
DEUTSCHE BANK	db.com/careers	ROYAL AIR FORCE	www.raf.mod.uk/recruitment
DLA PIPER	www.dlapipergraduates.com/uk	ROYAL NAVY	www.royalnavy.mod.uk/careers
DYSON	careers.dyson.com/early-careers	SANTANDER	www.santanderjobs.co.uk/realiseyourfuture
EXXONMOBIL	ExxonMobil.com/UKRecruitment	SAVILLS	savills.co.uk/graduates
EY	ukcareers.ey.com/graduates	SHELL	www.shell.co.uk/graduates
FRESHFIELDS BRUCKHAUS DERINGER	www.freshfields.com/ukgraduates	SIEMENS	siemens.co.uk/careers
FRONTLINE	www.thefrontline.org.uk	SKY	SkyEarlyCareers.com
GCHQ	www.gchq-careers.co.uk	SLAUGHTER AND MAY	www.slaughterandmay.com
GOLDMAN SACHS	goldmansachs.com/careers	TEACH FIRST	teachfirst.org.uk/graduates
GOOGLE	www.google.com/careers/students	TESCO	www.tesco-careers.com/graduates
GRANT THORNTON	trainees.grant-thornton.co.uk	THINK AHEAD	thinkahead.org
GSK	www.futureleaders.gsk.com	UNILEVER	www.unilever.co.uk/careers/graduates/uflp
HERBERT SMITH FREEHILLS	careers.herbertsmithfreehills.com/uk/grads	VIRGIN MEDIA	www.virginmediagraduates.co.uk
HOGAN LOVELLS	www.hoganlovells.com/graduates	WELLCOME	www.wellcome.ac.uk/graduates
HSBC	www.hsbc.com/careers/students-and-graduates	WHITE & CASE	www.whitecasetrainee.com
IBM	www.ibm.com/jobs/uk	WPP	www.wpp.com